UNITED KINGDOM
NATIONAL ENVIRONMENTAL HEALTH
ACTION PLAN

Presented to Parliament by the Secretaries of State for the Environment, for Northern Ireland, Health,

Scotland and Wales by Command of Her Majesty

July 1996

Contents

ANNEXES

List of Figures

Foreword

We have long recognised the environment to be a vital influence on health, even if it has not always been understood how this influence occurs. Since the Public Health Acts of the middle of the last century the basic components of environmental health – safe drinking water, sufficient food, good sanitation – have been established in this country. More recently we have also developed comprehensive systems for protecting health and the environment against pollution. Our understanding of the links between the environment and health has developed too. Life expectancy in the UK has greatly increased over the last hundred and fifty years, largely as a result of the combination of environmental health and medical advances.

Recognition of the significant impact that the quality of the environment can have on human health is a major part of our commitment to Agenda 21, the blueprint for sustainable development to which the UK and over 150 other nations pledged themselves at the Earth Summit in Rio de Janeiro in 1992. The Government's Sustainable Development Strategy develops that recognition into action. The annual Sustainable Development White Paper *This Common Inheritance* contains over 600 environmental commitments, many of which will be either directly or indirectly beneficial to the nation's health.

The National Environmental Health Action Plan takes the UK's commitment to environmental health and Agenda 21 another step forward. It contributes to the Environment and Health Action Plan for Europe, which was agreed at the Second European Conference on Environment and Health in Helsinki in 1994 by some 50 countries from across the European Region. It is the first such Action Plan to be published. In this the UK is playing a leading role as one of six pilot countries for the development of National Environmental Health Action Plans, providing experience to assist other countries in developing their own Action Plans. These Action Plans will provide a key focus for the Third European Environment and Health Conference, which will be hosted by the UK in London in 1999.

This Action Plan brings together the many facets of environmental health policy and provides an overview of plans for the future. As such it is a vital source document for public health professionals and the interested public alike. Many constructive comments emerged from the responses to the August 1995 public consultation document, and the Action Plan incorporates these in a similarly constructive fashion.

This document demonstrates that there is no single simple answer to a multitude of complex environmental health problems. Instead it provides a framework for actions by central and local government, industry and voluntary organisations, to improve the environment to the benefit of health. It points the way ahead, mapping the directions in which environmental health improvements are being constantly pushed forward.

We therefore present this National Environmental Health Action Plan as a guide to the next steps in improving environmental health in the UK. We believe that in keeping with Agenda 21 it will help involve everyone in promoting good environmental health for all.

JOHN GUMMER
Secretary of State
for the Environment

PATRICK MAYHEW
Secretary of State
for Northern Ireland

STEPHEN DORRELL
Secretary of State
for Health

MICHAEL FORSYTH
Secretary of State
for Scotland

WILLIAM HAGUE
Secretary of State
for Wales

Introduction and Background to the Plan

Scope and content of the plan

1. The Second European Conference on Environment and Health was held in Helsinki in June 1994. The Helsinki Conference was organised by the World Health Organisation Regional Office for Europe (WHO/EURO) in collaboration with the European Community.

2. Countries attending the Helsinki Conference committed themselves to developing national environmental health action plans. This United Kingdom National Environmental Health Action Plan (UK NEHAP), like the public consultation draft[143] published in August 1995, is based on a definition of environmental health, proposed to WHO in 1993:

> "Environmental health comprises those aspects of human health, including quality of life, that are determined by physical, biological, social and psychosocial factors in the environment. It also refers to the theory and practice of assessing, correcting, controlling and preventing those factors in the environment that can potentially affect adversely the health of present and future generations."

3. Against this definition the UK NEHAP describes:

- the institutional framework which underpins the regulatory and service provisions which ensure high and improving standards of environmental health;

- the management information systems which are essential to the rational assessment of hazards and rational measures based on sound science;

- how the various environmental pathways affect environmental health and how they are controlled for the benefit of environmental health;

- how too the home and working environments affect environmental health and how they are controlled for the benefit of environmental health;

- the interaction between major economic sectors and environmental health; and

- the UK's special international contribution to the improvement of environmental health.

In adopting this approach, the UK is deliberately following the format which WHO/EURO developed, with considerable assistance from the UK, as described in more detail below.

Historical background

4. The UK's environmental health programme was first given a legislative basis by the Public Health Act 1848. There followed a succession of Public Health and Sanitary Acts which defined the responsibilities of local authorities. From the 1850s onwards, the Alkali Acts were aimed at gross air pollution. The forerunners of today's environmental health officers were first appointed, with the title of 'sanitary inspectors', under the Public Health Act 1872.

5. Moving to this century, the Town and Country Planning Act 1947 remains the foundation of the present planning system. Among the other Acts which have been crucial to the steady improvement in environmental health in the UK are: the Public Health Act 1936; the Clean Air Acts of 1956 and 1968; the Health and Safety at Work Act 1974; the Control of Pollution Act 1974; the Environmental Protection Act 1990; and the Environment Act 1995.

6. Internationally, since the Stockholm Conference on the Human Environment in 1972, there has been continuing national and international concern with the environment and health and the interaction between them. In 1984, the Member States of WHO in the European Region set themselves 38 targets to be met by the year 2000 as part of the Health for All (HFA) strategy. In 1989, the First European Conference on Environment and Health was held in Frankfurt: it unanimously approved the European Charter on Environment and Health, which extends the European HFA strategy in its relation to the environment. The HFA targets, as updated in 1991[64], include eight environmental health targets which, with the target on accidents, express long-term policy environmental health objectives for Europe. The nine relevant targets are set out in Annex 3.

7. For the Helsinki Conference, WHO/EURO prepared a draft *Environmental Health Action Plan for Europe*[42] (EHAPE), which has since been finalised and published. The EHAPE set out a blueprint for the preparation of national environmental health action plans (NEHAPs) and a Europe-wide plan based on

them. The draft was subject to substantial review and comment by member states during its drafting before being endorsed at the Conference.

8. At the Helsinki Conference, the UK was represented by the Secretary of State for the Environment and the Minister for Health. The *Declaration*[31] issued by the Ministers of member states and by others attending the conference said:

> "We endorse the Environmental Health Action Plan for Europe (EHAPE) as the means through which we may protect and promote health and conserve and improve the environment. We are committed to implementing its major thrusts, as follows:

> "We commit our respective health and environment departments to developing jointly, not later than 1997, action plans on health and the environment, working with and through competent authorities or inviting them to draw up such action plans where appropriate and legally or constitutionally required. These plans should be integrated in or closely linked with both environmental action programmes and with health planning processes, and specifically the action plans required by the UNCED follow-up and the Environment for Europe process. We will intensify cooperation with other governmental authorities, such as those responsible for agriculture, energy, industry, transport and tourism, in order to integrate environmental and health issues into their existing policies, as an important step towards sustainability."

9. The UK NEHAP is both a national plan and a response to that commitment. It builds upon the work done by WHO/EURO in preparing the EHAPE blueprint. The UK NEHAP and the plans of other countries will feed into a European plan which is expected to be the focus of the Third European Conference on Environment and Health which the UK will host in 1999.

Immediate antecedents

10. On 2 August 1995, the Secretary of State for the Environment, John Gummer, and the Secretary of State for Health, Stephen Dorrell, published the draft[143] of the UK NEHAP. The plan remained open for consultation until 27 October 1995. Announcing the consultation, the hope was expressed that

> "... publication of the draft will enable a wide range of people to contribute to the consultation process and to the setting of priorities which will result."

In the event, nearly 250 people and organisations responded to the invitation to comment. The replies included many constructive criticisms which have been taken into account in this plan.

11. An effective plan for environmental health must alter in a dynamic and responsive way to changing circumstances. Therefore, the UK NEHAP presented here is no more and should be no more than a current plan. Just as the UK's response to the Sustainable Development Strategy and the UK's Environment Strategy is monitored and revised with new targets in, for example, *This Common Inheritance: UK Annual Report 1995*[139], so the actions in the UK NEHAP will be revised from time to time to take account of changed circumstances and new knowledge.

Integrated policies

12. There is a range of influences on individual health status including heredity, economic circumstances, lifestyle and environment. Environmental health factors amount to only part of the many interacting influences which need to be taken into account when considering action to promote human health and wellbeing.

13. The concept of 'environmental health' encompasses domestic, leisure and workplace and each of these, in turn, has many components. Although environmental health is a holistic discipline, its many contributory factors are so disparate that they must be considered separately before they can be considered as a whole. Moreover, an action plan for environmental health cannot stand alone. The whole plan, and its component parts, must be related to, and integrated with, plans to meet other needs of the community: for example, employment and leisure; economy and development. An environmental health action plan must be a multi-disciplinary effort.

14. Additionally, a NEHAP must take account of preexisting, separate, plans relevant to environment and health and of how such plans fit in with international initiatives. Examples of such plans are *Sustainable Development – The UK Strategy*[133] and the health policy statement for each of the UK countries, such as *The Health of the Nation – A Strategy for Health in England*[65]. An example of an international initiative is the European Union (EU) Sustainable Cities Campaign. Moreover, the fundamental principles underlying such plans and initiatives will continue to be applicable to this plan.

15. A further complicating factor is the number of organisations whose activities give them an interest in environmental health. The actions of individuals and of organisations, large and small, may have an impact

on aspects of environmental health; and those actions may impact, for better or worse, on the general public at an immediate local or a much wider level. The Government invited comment on the public consultation draft of the UK NEHAP from the community at all levels, voluntary organisations, industry, local government and learned societies to ensure that the current plan reflects and addresses the most pressing concerns and that it commands commitment to its implementation.

Format of the plans

16. In developing the UK NEHAP, the UK has followed the EHAPE format which we helped WHO/ EURO to develop. The principal alternative was to address directly the nine HFA targets (para 6 above). After consideration of the issues described under 'Integrated policies' (paras 12-15 above), the EHAPE model was chosen as the best way forward: an approach based on more generalised objectives would have been difficult to relate to the institutional and legal framework of the UK.

17. The UK has made two additions to the EHAPE format:

(i) a new section '3.7 Noise' for which the UK has framed its own objective; and

(ii) Chapter 6 International Action which deals with those specific UK contributions to the international effort that go beyond the normal participation in international institutions.

The first of these is a direct response to a point made in the public consultation process.

18. For each of the areas under consideration, under the heading:

– **Objectives**, the UK NEHAP repeats word for word the objectives of the EHAPE;

– **Basis for action**, the current position in the UK is described; and

– **Actions**, proposed actions are recorded under the appropriate group number as described in para 19 below.

In endorsing the Helsinki *Declaration*[31] the UK broadly accepted the objectives set out in the EHAPE. The Helsinki Conference accepted that the various countries of Europe differ in how close they are to reaching or exceeding those objectives; in the priorities they attach to them; and in how differences will be reflected in their separate NEHAPs.

19. The UK NEHAP classifies levels of action using the same three groups as the EHAPE:

"*Group 1* actions concern the basic requirements for environmental health. They aim at preventing or mitigating conditions whose environmental causes are well established and can give rise to widespread and often acute health effects. The conditions would worsen with time if not brought under control. Control may yield immediate benefits, roughly in proportion to the magnitude of the investment, that will be easily recognizable by the public. In addition, most such control measures are technically feasible at reasonable costs.

"*Group 2* actions concern the prevention and control of medium- and long-term environmental health hazards. Causal relationships may be more difficult to establish at existing environmental concentrations, but the potential for adverse effects on health is recognized. They include long-term effects from both chronic and shorter-term exposures; some of these may be irreversible effects, associated, for example, with increased cancer risks. The benefits of the action may only appear after many years, although when the actions lead to rapid and marked reductions of air and water pollution, their value will be rapidly appreciated by the public.

"*Group 3* actions concern the promotion of human wellbeing and mental health rather than the prevention of disease. Perception of the environment as unpleasant imposes stress on the affected population. Different factors may be perceived as unpleasant by different groups of people, and so considerable expense could be entailed in attempting to satisfy everybody. Thus, even more than with Group 2 actions, priority-setting is crucial here to ensure the most effective investment of resources. Since such priority-setting will involve considerations of public perception, public education and information are essential if the limited funds available are to be invested appropriately. Public willingness to pay is also relevant. On the other hand, a good environment can enhance the quality of life. Environmental planning can support the formation of local social networks. Involvement of communities in planning and maintaining their surroundings will increase awareness of the long-term benefits for health and wellbeing of measures to protect the environment."

20. Commenting on these groups, the EHAPE says:

"Common to all groups is the consideration that, because some environmental improvements may be expensive and their impact on health uncertain or difficult to quantify, countries need to consider carefully how far they can afford each element, having regard to its cost and likely yield in terms of gain to health or wellbeing."

Setting priorities

21. An essential prerequisite to determining, and committing a country to, actions is to identify:

- actual or potential hazards to health in the environment;

- the impacts on health which those hazards may cause;

- the degree of priority with which each should be addressed;

- the relative costs and benefits of action; and

- where resources are constrained, the most cost-effective action.

22. Planning for action on environmental hazards needs to focus first on identification and recognition of the hazards and their associated risks to public health. This may be a relatively simple process reflecting well-established scientific evidence from other areas or other countries. In such cases, prioritisation will take that evidence and build upon it, reflecting national and more local circumstances, the extent and severity of adverse health effects, and the resources which can be made available to reduce or remove the hazard.

23. Where environmental conditions present a serious hazard to public health (whether in terms of the number of people affected or of the severity of the effect), the ideal objective is the complete removal of the hazard; but in some cases this will not be possible – either at all or at least in the short-term – and the priority will then be to reduce the risks and to plan, over a reasonable period of time, to remove them where this is technically possible.

24. As action plans are developed, implemented and rolled forward, priority-setting becomes an iterative process; environmental conditions and public health states are monitored; as changes occur, and scientific understanding is gained and developed, priorities will change and be updated to reflect the impact of earlier actions and the need to address other, or new, risks. The present UK NEHAP is a snapshot of what has long been and will continue to be an ongoing process.

The pilot project

25. Because Ministers at the Helsinki Conference attached such importance to the development of

NEHAPs, WHO/EURO decided to start a pilot project with six countries to:

- obtain practical experience in the making of such plans;

- disseminate the lessons learned; and, thereby,

- help other member states develop their NEHAPs.

26. The Government accepted the invitation from WHO/EURO to participate as one of the six pilot countries: they were chosen to have a geographic spread and a range of economic circumstances. The other pilot countries are Bulgaria, Hungary, Italy, Latvia and Uzbekistan. The pilot countries all committed themselves to complete their NEHAPs by mid 1996 and to cooperate with each other with a view to achieving a successful outcome.

27. At their first meeting, held in Budapest in January 1995, the other pilot countries agreed that the EHAPE model was suitable and that the pilot project would be most useful to other countries if the pilot countries' plans followed its format. Details of how the pilot project has developed are given in Annex 7.

The UK NEHAP

28. The UK NEHAP:

- gives both an overview of the provision of environmental health and a detailed analysis of the many factors contributing to it;

- shows how the current provisions will deliver a steady improvement in environmental health or how they should be modified to do so;

- sets out a range of well over 150 specific actions across the spectrum of environmental health for remedying identified problems or for securing further improvements; and, thereby,

- establishes the means to achieve the objectives of the Environmental Health Action Plan for Europe and the Health for All targets.

Progress in implementing the plan will be reported from time to time in Departmental publications.

29. Additionally, the UK NEHAP, and the processes leading to it, will act as a guide for the formulation of similar environmental health action plans in other European countries.

1 Institutional Framework

Objectives

- To ensure, through the establishment of appropriate government machinery, that decisions and long-term strategic planning affecting the natural environment, and through it health, are taken not merely on the basis of economic factors alone but also with full consideration of potential environmental health consequences, in accordance with the requirements of sustainable development.

- Similarly, to ensure that decisions on economic development at local level are taken in full knowledge of their environmental implications and potential consequences for health, through effective consultation involving not only local authorities and those who stand to benefit financially from the proposed development but also the population that will be affected by the positive or negative outcomes of the decision.

(EHAPE para 68)

Basis for action

Definitions

1. The above objectives contain two terms which are fundamental to the whole plan, namely, 'environmental health' and 'sustainable development'. The definition of **environmental health**, used for this plan was given in the Introduction (para 2). The definition of **sustainable development** is the one used in the UK's sustainable development strategy[133], taken from *Our Common Future*[88]:

> "development that meets the needs of the present without compromising the ability of future generations to meet their own needs".

The principal players

2. In the UK, the principal players ensuring full consideration of environmental health consequences of decisions are:

> (i)   the Government and its Departments;
>
> (ii) the Health and Safety Commission and Executive;
>
> (iii) the Environment Agencies;
>
> (iv) the Royal Commission on Environmental Pollution (RCEP);
>
> (v)   local authorities; and
>
> (vi) regulators of certain industries.

The Government and its Departments

3. Sustainable development which aims to reconcile economic development and environmental protection is essential for the long term protection of health. If the 'green message' is to be promoted effectively, there must be commitment to it across Government. The long tradition of collective Cabinet responsibility means that the UK has well-established methods for ensuring coordination of policy across Government. These were enhanced in 1993 to ensure effective consideration of sustainable development policy.

4. Annual environment White Papers are presented to Parliament; these are agreed by all Government Departments and now describe progress in meeting the UK's sustainable development and other environmental commitments. As an example, *This Common Inheritance, UK Annual Report 1995*[139] recorded the state of play on over 600 commitments. The process offers a powerful tool to encourage all of Government to keep up to the mark.

5. Environmental policy, much of which is fundamental to environmental health policy, is integrated into the work of all Government Departments in a number of other ways:

- Cabinet Committees on the Environment and on Health provide a forum for Ministers to consider key issues concerning the environment and health respectively. Issues relevant to environmental health may be raised and discussed in either Committee. Any policy proposals going before Cabinet or Ministerial Committees must be accompanied by an assessment of environmental costs and benefits where these are significant;

- the UK has set up consultative committees with industry, local government and the voluntary sector;

- in all Departments, a 'Green Minister' has been appointed whose job it is to ensure that environmental considerations are integrated into the strategy and policies of his or her own department. They are supported by a network of 'green contacts' at official level across all Departments to develop best practice and coordinate policy;

- each Government Department now includes in its own Annual Report material on that Department's environmental performance; and

- all Government Departments now have strategies in place for good environmental housekeeping.

6. The UK sustainable development strategy[133] recognised that much of the early UK environmental legislation was motivated by a concern to protect human health – by curbing air pollution, providing clean water and minimising risks from waste disposal. Although constant watchfulness is needed to avoid pollution which may cause acute health incidents, such incidents are now rare. Consequently, public concern today centres on health issues where it is harder to identify the strength of linkages between cause or possible cause and effect.

7. The Government has always recognised that the task of achieving sustainable development involves the whole country – central and local government, business, other organisations and individuals. Ultimately it depends upon the choices about their lifestyles made by every member of society. Accordingly, wide consultation was at the heart of the production of the sustainable development strategy and remains vital to its continuing implementation.

8. Alongside existing machinery, such as public consultation on planning issues, Parliamentary Select Committees and the RCEP, the UK set up new mechanisms:

- five very eminent specialists were appointed by the Prime Minister to a Government Panel on Sustainable Development to advise and monitor progress;

- a UK Round Table on Sustainable Development of 35 representatives of various sectors and groups is reviewing the issues and considering how to achieve greater consensus across society about how to tackle them;

- 'Going for Green' is working with existing promotional groups to get the message of

sustainable development across to individuals in their private lives; and

- in Scotland, the Secretary of State has established an Advisory Group to address the distinct challenges and implications for Scotland in tackling sustainable development and to provide independent advice to Scottish Ministers on the issues.

9. For many matters, the Secretaries of State for Northern Ireland, Scotland and Wales each have powers and responsibilities for their own regions which mirror those of more than one Secretary of State, each responsible for a specific aspect (for example, environment, health) in England. The responsibilities of Departments for the separate aspects of environmental health are set out in Annex 5. Later sections of this plan will take account of any such differences that are significant. The Secretaries of State are supported by their respective offices: the Northern Ireland Office (NIO), the Scottish Office (SO) and the Welsh Office (WO).

The Health and Safety Commission and Executive

10. The Health and Safety Commission (HSC) and Health and Safety Executive (HSE) are statutory bodies whose aims are to protect the health, safety and welfare of employees, and to safeguard others, principally the public, who may be exposed to risks from industrial activity.

11. HSC is responsible to the Secretary of State for Environment, and other Secretaries of State, for the administration of the Health and Safety at Work etc. Act 1974. HSE is a distinct statutory body which advises and assists HSC, and has day to day responsibility for enforcing health and safety legislation. This work includes providing a framework of law and standards; protecting workers and the public from risks of accidents and to their health through inspection and assessment of hazardous processes and plant; investigation of accidents, cases of ill-health and complaints about working conditions. The role of HSC and HSE in relation to occupational health is described in more detail in Section 4.2.

12. The Health and Safety Commission and Executive have a comprehensive consultation procedure, including an extensive system of expert advisory committees which are subject or industry based. This includes an Occupational Health Advisory Committee which considers and advises HSC on:

- encouraging systems for managing health at work;

- developing occupational health services and competencies;

- improving data on occupational disease; and

- promoting health in the workplace.

The Environment Agencies

13. From 1 April 1996, the following aspects of operation of pollution control became the responsibility of three new agencies:

> in England and Wales, the Environment Agency (EA), a new non-departmental public body, took over the functions of Her Majesty's Inspectorate of Pollution (HMIP), the National Rivers Authority (NRA) and the local waste regulation authorities, including significant responsibilities for water management as well as pollution control;
>
> in Scotland, the Scottish Environment Protection Agency (SEPA), a new non-departmental public body, took over the functions of Her Majesty's Industrial Pollution Inspectorate (HMIPI), river purification authorities, local waste regulation authorities, the Hazardous Waste Inspectorate, and local authorities under Part I of the Environmental Protection Act 1990; and
>
> in Northern Ireland, the Environment and Heritage Service (a Next Steps Agency of the Department of the Environment for Northern Ireland (DOENI)) became responsible for the control of air pollution from major industrial sources and for water pollution control.

14. The greater integration means that the Agencies are better placed than the predecessor bodies to: consider the environment as a whole, rather than air, water and land in isolation; deliver a consistent approach to regulation; and provide a more streamlined service to industry and the public.

Royal Commission on Environmental Pollution

15. In 1970, the RCEP was established. It is an independent standing body which advises on environmental issues in accordance with the following terms of reference:

> To advise on matters, both national and international, concerning the pollution of the environment; on the adequacy of research in this field; and the future possibilities of danger to the environment.

16. The RCEP has freedom to consider and advise on any matter it chooses: the Government may also request the RCEP to consider particular topics. It has published reports on a wide variety of environmental topics, most of them relevant to environmental health: for instance, in 1994 it studied transport and in 1996 soil.

Local authorities

17. Local authorities have a key role in the provision of environmental health services. Annex 5 describes the structure of local government within the UK, what environmental health services are provided by it, and how. As will become evident in later sections of the plan, local authorities will have a key role, with Government, in the implementation of the UK NEHAP.

18. Local authorities already have experience of developing local plans within an overall national policy. Following the 1992 United Nations Conference on the Environment and Development (UNCED) – the Rio Earth Summit – and the 1994 Global Forum, the UK developed its sustainable development strategy[133] (para 6 above). Local authorities are carrying forward their own programme of work on sustainable development within that framework through the 'Local Agenda 21' initiative.

19. In many cases it will be appropriate for local authorities to develop a local environmental health action plan (LEHAP) because so many environmental health decisions are best taken at the local level to reflect local circumstances and local priorities. The Government will encourage them to do so within the framework set by the UK NEHAP.

20. A pilot Capital Challenge scheme invites local authorities to compete for £600m of credit approvals available in the three years from 1 April 1997 by bringing forward their highest priority projects for capital investment across all services which they provide. Environmental health projects are eligible for support.

Local authorities and the planning system

21. Through the planning system, local authorities have powers to regulate the development and use of land in the public interest, helping thereby to promote environmental health. All local authorities must prepare land use development plans. Planning decisions must accord with the development plan unless material considerations indicate otherwise. It is important, therefore, that local people and organisations involve themselves in the plan preparation process. They have the right to be consulted by the local planning authority and so

formally object, if necessary before an independent inspector. In Northern Ireland, there are similar arrangements but the responsibility for land use rests with the DoENI.

22. The Government (through the Department of the Environment (DoE), SO and WO) issues planning policy guidance on planning policies and the operation of the planning system. Since the publication in 1990 of the White Paper *This Common Inheritance*[138], the Government has undertaken a comprehensive revision and review of all planning guidance to reflect environmental priorities set out in the strategy. The review has resulted in a series of Policy Planning Guidance Notes such as those on *Transport*[91], *Planning and Noise*[93], and *Planning Guidance (Wales) Planning Policy*[90] which sets out the Government's land use policies as they apply to Wales and will be supplemented by a series of Technical Advice Notes. Local authorities must take Government policy into account when preparing their development plans, so development control decisions will reflect the principles of sustainable development.

23. Policies for land use must weigh and coordinate priorities in the public interest. One such priority is a physically safe environment. Planning helps to ensure for example that proper precautions are taken against the risks of coastal erosion, flooding, subsidence and incidents at major chemical installations. Plans must also include policies to control pollution, to protect water quality, to limit and reduce nuisances such as noise, smells and dirt. They must also include policies to reduce air pollution through transport policies that reduce the need to travel, particularly by private car.

Regulators

24. In England, Scotland and Wales the electricity and gas supply industries are in the private sector. In England and Wales, water services are also in the private sector. For each industry there is a Government appointed Regulator charged with overseeing the industry to protect the public from abuse of monopoly power. The role of the Regulator in relation to environmental health factors is explained in the relevant sections: Section 3.1 – Water; and Section 5.2 – Energy.

25. The role of the National Meat Hygiene Agency in relation to food is dealt with in Section 3.3 – Food.

Actions: Group 3

26. The following Group 3 actions are planned:

(1) In such regular reports as the series *This Common Inheritance*, the Government will report on progress on UK NEHAP targets and commitments, and update them from time to time, on a continuing basis.

(2) For the institutional framework, the normal process of continual review will remain, ensuring that new mechanisms will be established as necessary.

(3) At the request of Green Ministers, DoE will publish a series of case studies to show that environmental considerations are being taken into account in policies and programmes of Government Departments.

(4) For Northern Ireland, legislation will be introduced in 1996 to transfer waste disposal regulation powers to the Environment and Heritage Service.

2 Environmental Health Management Tools

2.1 Environment and Health Information Systems

Objectives

- To improve the relevance, quality and availability of data on various aspects of the environment related to health (eg pollutant levels in air, water, soil, food, body fluids and tissues) for purposes of situation, trend and impact analysis, as required for national environmental policy development and evaluation, as well as for research purposes.

- For the same purposes as above, to improve the value of mortality and morbidity data by making them accessible at suitably low levels of geographic aggregation and by facilitating the possibility of relating them to environmental and other external factors (eg occupation, lifestyle) that may contribute to mortality, morbidity or both.

- To develop country-specific environmental health profiles as the basis for defining priorities for action and for monitoring progress.

(EHAPE para 79)

Basis for action

Introduction

1. These are not easy objectives. Given unlimited resources, there is no particular difficulty in monitoring the quality of the environment in relation to specific pollutants or the state of the public health in relation to specific illnesses. There **is** difficulty in relating the one to the other with sound scientific evidence which will support a case for action and the resource implications of that action – and no country has unlimited resources with which to address that difficulty.

2. There are many causes of ill-health, which may inter-relate one with another and the effects of which may vary because of the particular circumstances of individual people, including the conditions in which they are exposed to the 'cause'. Consequently, it is very difficult to identify a particular illness and to state, with confidence, that it is principally caused by a particular condition of the environment. It is equally difficult to identify a particular environmental condition and to state, with confidence, that it is the principal cause of a particular condition of ill-health. These difficulties may be reduced where there is gross pollution and obvious ill-health but are greatly exacerbated when – as is commonly the case in the UK – people's exposure to a potential health hazard, or combination of potential hazards, is very low.

3. What can be done to meet these objectives is to monitor both the state of the environment and the state of the public health and to seek, through epidemiological and other research, to improve our understanding of the effects of the environment upon health. Being realistic about the availability of resources, that monitoring must reflect national and more local priorities, founded on scientific evidence, for environmental conditions, public health and the possible link between the two.

4. DoE has a project underway to mount a wide range of data sets on the state of the environment on to the World Wide Web of the Internet. A pilot version, based on data from the *Digest of Environmental Statistics No 17*[32] (the *Digest*) published in April 1995, became available in mid 1996 and a live version, based on *Digest No 18*, is expected to be available in late summer 1996. The range of DoE environmental statistics publications has recently been enhanced with the publication in March 1996 of a preliminary set of *Indicators of Sustainable Development for the United Kingdom*[73]. Information from this publication will be mounted on the Internet in the second half of 1996. Both initiatives will help to widen the availability of environmental information and also to make it easier for users, both in the UK and abroad, to access and manipulate data for analysis. In addition, the environmental statistics for Scotland are published biennially by the SO in *The Scottish Environment: Statistics.*

5. Local authorities' Environmental Health Departments undertake a wide range of environmental monitoring including air pollution, freshwater quality, bathing waters, radioactivity, noise and derelict land. Much of the information gathering is to meet local needs eg freshwaters and bathing waters, or as part of national surveys eg Derelict Land Surveys for England. In most cases there are no statutory requirements for collection of these data. As a result, data are often collected for different purposes using different sampling methodologies etc, and therefore it is not always possible to provide a meaningful national picture owing to lack of comparability.

6. A number of local authorities, for example Lancashire County Council and Kirklees Metropolitan District Council, produce state of the environment reports, which include results from their environmental monitoring activities. More recently, attention has focused on producing key local sustainability indicators. The Local Government Management Board has been investigating ways of developing such indicators as part of the Local Agenda 21 process, and the results of a pilot project were published by the Local Government Management Board in 1995[136]. It is likely that more local authorities will take up the challenge of producing key sustainability indicators in future. More generally, the Environmental Statistics Sub-Group of the Information Development Liaison Group, a body which co-ordinates national and local government statistical interests, is concentrating on trying to improve harmonisation of locally collected environmental data and on the integration of local and national indicators of sustainable development.

Water quality

7. Water quality is monitored throughout the country and reported in the *Digest*[32]. Drinking water quality is measured against a prescribed concentration or value for a range of parameters, including coliforms, metals and pesticides, and annual results are published by the Drinking Water Inspectorate[33] (DWI) and by the SO[34] and reported in summary tables in the *Digest*. The quality of waters for fish is monitored under the European Commission's (EC) Freshwater Fish Directive by the EA in England and Wales, and by the SEPA in Scotland, and by the Environment and Heritage Service of DoENI in Northern Ireland. The *Digest* reports the overall compliance level against the mandatory requirements set for the physical and chemical parameters.

Bathing waters

8. Results of the sampling of bathing waters for physical, chemical and microbiological parameters for the EC Bathing Water Directive[172] are held on a database by DoE and published annually by the NRA, by DoE in a Report to Parliament, and in the *Digest*[32] and reported also to the EC. The *Digest* not only gives detailed results for the latest year but also makes some comparisons with previous years to show trends. The SO also publishes results annually.

Air quality

9. There are, in the current UK monitoring program, over 60 automatic air monitoring stations throughout the country, together with over 1400 sampler measurement sites. These are organised into three automatic networks (Urban, Hydrocarbon and Rural) and six sampler-based programmes (diffusion tube, smoke/SO_2, lead and multi-element, acid deposition, rural SO_2 and toxic organic micropollutants). All pollutants are measured in the light of national and EC Directive standards and WHO guidelines.

10. The Automated Urban and Rural Networks are used to fulfil the UK's compliance with the EC nitrogen dioxide and ozone Directives. The Automated Urban Network currently comprises sites which monitor sulphur dioxide, nitrogen dioxide, carbon monoxide, ozone and fine particulate matter (PM_{10}) concentrations at a variety of urban locations, ranging from kerbside and industrial monitoring to monitoring urban background areas representative of air pollution exposure for large numbers of people. This network is being expanded and, by the end of 1996, will include over 80 sites and provide a comprehensive coverage of air quality in UK cities.

11. All the data referred to in the previous paragraph are published in the *Digest*[32]. Hourly bulletins on levels of ambient SO_2, NO_2, O_3, benzene and 1,3-butadiene are available to the public together with an air quality forecast via a free telephone line (0800-556677); Teletext page 106; CEEFAX page 404); and other media, including national and local TV, radio and newspapers. Hourly bulletins on levels of ambient SO_2, NO_2, O_3, benzene, 1,3-butadiene, CO and PM_{10} are also available on the Internet (address http://www.open.gov.uk/doe/doehome.htm). The first set of Air Quality Indicators was published in *Indicators of Sustainable Development for the United Kingdom*[73].

Figure 1 UK automated air quality monitoring sites: March 1995

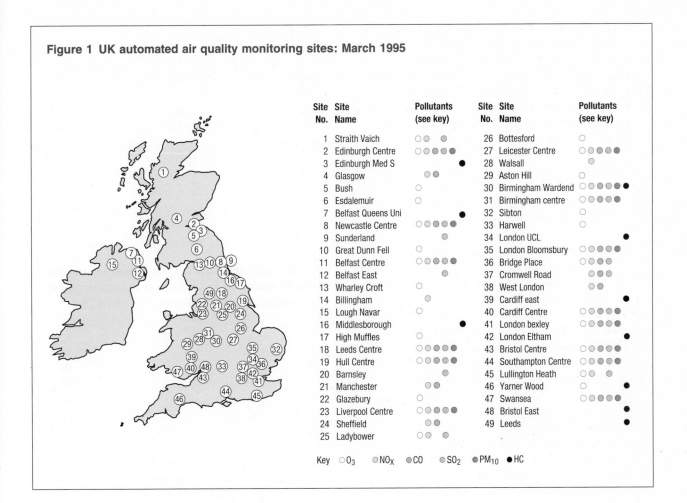

Site No.	Site Name	Pollutants (see key)	Site No.	Site Name	Pollutants (see key)
1	Straith Vaich	○○ ●	26	Bottesford	○
2	Edinburgh Centre	○○●●●	27	Leicester Centre	○○●●●
3	Edinburgh Med S	●	28	Walsall	●
4	Glasgow	○●	29	Aston Hill	○
5	Bush	○	30	Birmingham Wardend	○○●●●●
6	Esdalemuir	○	31	Birmingham centre	○○●●●
7	Belfast Queens Uni	●	32	Sibton	○
8	Newcastle Centre	○○●●●	33	Harwell	○
9	Sunderland	●	34	London UCL	●
10	Great Dunn Fell	○	35	London Bloomsbury	○○●●●
11	Belfast Centre	○○●●●	36	Bridge Place	○●●●
12	Belfast East	●	37	Cromwell Road	○●●
13	Wharley Croft	○	38	West London	○●
14	Billingham	●	39	Cardiff east	●
15	Lough Navar	○	40	Cardiff Centre	○○●●●
16	Middlesborough	●	41	London bexley	○○●●●
17	High Muffles	○	42	London Eltham	●
18	Leeds Centre	○○●●●	43	Bristol Centre	○○●●●
19	Hull Centre	○○●●●	44	Southampton Centre	○○●●●
20	Barnsley	●	45	Lullington Heath	○○ ●
21	Manchester	○●	46	Yarner Wood	○ ●
22	Glazebury	○	47	Swansea	○○●●●
23	Liverpool Centre	○○●●●	48	Bristol East	●
24	Sheffield	○●	49	Leeds	●
25	Ladybower	○○ ●			

Key ○ O₃   ○ NOₓ   ● CO   ● SO₂   ● PM₁₀   ● HC

12. The *Digest* has data for Wales and the WO also publishes an annual *Environment Digest for Wales*[41] providing environmental statistics. In addition, a Wales Air Quality Forum has been set up to coordinate monitoring results obtained by local authorities.

Food

13. The Government's microbiological food safety surveillance and assessment system is co-ordinated at the national level by the Microbiological Food Surveillance Group (MFSG) in conjunction with the Advisory Committee on the Microbiological Safety of Food (ACMSF). The objective of the MFSG is to co-ordinate surveillance activities and identify through surveillance the need for action to ensure the microbiological safety of food. The ACMSF provides the Government with expert advice on microbiological food safety and advises the Government on its food safety surveillance and research programme. This programme complements surveillance activities undertaken at local level by local authorities in conjunction with the Public Health Laboratory Service (PHLS).

14. The PHLS collects data on incidents of foodborne disease from laboratory reports and outbreak investigations, and assists local authorities and the National Health Service (NHS) in managing outbreaks. The Office of National Statistics (ONS) collects data on reported cases of food poisoning (which includes illness caused by microbiological and chemical contamination). The Government is advised by the ACMSF on the national impact of epidemiological data.

15. The Government's food surveillance programme covers the whole food chain from raw materials through manufacture and processing to subsequent storage and distribution of the food. Eleven Working Parties organise a wide range of food surveillance activities and related research in areas ranging from nutrients to inorganic contaminants in food. Their surveillance programmes are coordinated so as to contribute to the Ministry of Agriculture, Fisheries and Food's (MAFF) aim of ensuring a safe, nutritious and authentic food supply. Data on the nature, level and incidence of contaminants in foodstuffs form the basis for advice to Government and recommendations for action as necessary.

16. The concentrations of contaminants such as mercury, copper, dieldrin and polychlorinated biphenyls (PCBs) measured in fish and shellfish off the coast of the UK are collected by the Directorate of

Fisheries Research of MAFF and published in its *Aquatic Environment Monitoring Reports*[10] and also summarised in the *Digest*[32].

17. Results from the pesticides and radionuclides programme are published annually. Pesticide residue analyses are conducted mainly as rolling programmes carried out at 1–5 year intervals depending on the foodstuff. Methods capable of determining wide ranges of pesticide residues are used wherever possible to ensure that the maximum amount of information on residues present per analysis is obtained. For the other programmes, completed surveys are announced monthly in the Food Safety Directorate Information Bulletin and an explanatory note on each individual survey is available on request from MAFF. The reports of such surveys are lodged in the library of the Department of Health (DH) for public access. In addition, the results of the Working Parties have been published as Food Surveillance Papers. Some Working Parties also produce annual reports and there is an overall annual report[128] describing the achievements of the surveillance programme and summarising the work carried out by each of the eleven Working Parties during the year.

18. In all, approximately 100,500 analyses were made during 1995, subdivided as follows:

inorganic contaminants	7,200
organic contaminants	6,700
pesticides	70,000
radionuclides	16,600

19. The Annual Report[137] of the Terrestrial Radioactivity Monitoring Programme (TRAMP) includes assessments of doses to critical groups from consumption of food and agricultural products derived from sites near nuclear establishments and a summary of maximum doses to critical groups from consumption of these foodstuffs based on these reports is published as a table in the *Digest*[32]. Measurements of concentrations of strontium-90 and caesium-137 in milk from farms near nuclear establishments are also taken by British Nuclear Fuels PLC (BNFL) and the UK Atomic Energy Authority (UKAEA) and these too are published in the *Digest*. More detailed figures relating to Scotland are published by SO in a statistical bulletin[127]. Nuclear operators (eg BNFL, UKAEA, Nuclear Electric) produce their own annual reports which give monitoring information on discharges and exposure of the public to radiation in the vicinity of nuclear sites.

20. MAFF also carries out a programme of monitoring radioactivity in the aquatic environment to assess the impacts of discharges in fresh and marine waters. These results also are reported annually in the *Aquatic Environment Monitoring Reports*[10]

Solid wastes and soil pollution

21. In 1995, the DoE and the WO jointly published a White Paper (Cm 3040) *Making Waste Work: A strategy for sustainable waste management in England and Wales*[79]. A central plank of the White Paper is the development of a data strategy to ensure that waste management decisions are based on sound information about the sources, amounts and types of controlled and other wastes, and about what proportions of waste are recycled, composted, incinerated or landfilled, and how these are changing over time. DoE has published details of its waste management information requirements and recommendations for improving the quality of the available data. The report provides the framework for the development of the data strategy. A special new task force has been set up within DoE to take forward the recommendations of the review report and to liaise with the new Environment Agencies in collecting and providing waste information.

22. Soil is a complex environmental medium for which monitoring activities are not as extensive as for other environmental media, eg air and water. The most recent comprehensive inventory of soils was undertaken for the National Soils Inventory (NSI) of England and Wales in 1979-81. Partial re-sampling of the NSI sites was undertaken in 1995 and some results are presented in the preliminary set of *Indicators of Sustainable Development for the United Kingdom*[73].

23. The RCEP has recently undertaken a study into environmental problems associated with soils. The RCEP's report, *Sustainable Use of Soils*[135], which was published in February 1996, makes 91 recommendations covering all aspects of soil use. The Government is currently considering the recommendations and will publish a formal response.

24. The Environment Act 1995 made provision for new legislation on contaminated land. When introduced, this legislation will, among other things, require local authorities to inspect their land from time to time to identify contaminated sites, to determine the works needed to make the land suitable for use, and to keep registers of sites that have been and are being remediated. The Environment Agencies will be responsible for certain sites, and are required to publish reports setting out the extent of contaminated land.

25. The European Environment Agency (EEA) in Copenhagen is to establish a European Topic Centre (ETC) for Soils in 1996. The ETC will be tasked with improving data on soil at the European level to assist policy making in the European Union and in Member States. Among the tasks of the ETC will be to develop suitable indicators for soil.

Radioactivity

26. For levels of radioactivity relevant to health, estimates of the overall radiation exposure of the UK population to discharges from sites handling radioactivity, together with estimates of exposure from other sources, are reviewed[102] by the National Radiological Protection Board (NRPB) and published in tabular form in the *Digest*[32]. Information on radon levels in houses, derived from surveys[49] undertaken by the NRPB, has been included in recent editions of the *Digest*. The EA and SEPA have inherited from HMIP and HMIPI responsibility for monitoring radioactivity in the environment which might lead to exposure to the public from non food pathways. A similar responsibility is discharged in Northern Ireland by the Environment and Heritage Service of DoENI. MAFF have responsibility for monitoring the disposal and discharge of radioactive wastes from nuclear sites where this might lead to exposure of the public via the food chain.

27. Raw drinking water sources are monitored, against guideline values set by WHO, for levels of radioactivity by analysis of samples by the water companies. Again these results appear, in summary, in the *Digest*.

Nuclear accidents

28. Monitoring of levels of radioactivity in the environment would be necessary following a nuclear accident to aid decisions on, for example, decontamination and relocation. A number of Government Departments and other bodies are capable of carrying out such monitoring which would be coordinated at the local level and supported by the relevant lead Government Department. The aim is to find a standard way of presenting data to the best effect for any nuclear accident.

Noise

29. Statistics on noise complaints are collated annually by the Chartered Institute for Environmental Health (CIEH). These data, together with other noise statistics, appear in the *Digest*[32]. Summary data on the effects of noise from a Survey[36] of national attitudes to noise were presented in the 1995 *Digest*. Results of a National Noise Incidence Study[85] concluded that over half the homes in England and Wales were exposed to noise levels outside the home exceeding the WHO level of 55 dB $L_{Aeq, T}$ chosen to prevent significant community annoyance.

Environment and health generally

30. General information on environment and health is published in a chapter of *The UK Environment*[143], a statistical work aimed at the more general reader. Subjects discussed within the chapter for their possible influences on health included: lead, other metals, dioxins, pesticides, sewage, radioactivity and noise. Cross-references were made to other chapters in the book.

31. The Environmental Statistics Advisory Group (ESAG), comprising representatives from within government organisations and from non-governmental groups involved in the environmental arena, was set up in 1994 by DoE to provide advice on the collection and presentation of official statistics. It meets twice a year.

32. In some parts of England and in Wales, surveillance data on health aspects of acute chemical contamination incidents is collected by collaborative groups drawn from Health Authorities, Local Authorities and other institutions. Examples include work by the All-Wales Environmental Health Surveillance Project, the West Midlands Regional Advisory Group on Chemical Contamination Incidents, and the Chemical Incident Research Programme at the Medical Toxicology Unit of the Guy's and St Thomas' Hospital Trust. *Ad hoc* surveys are also undertaken. The development of such systems is evolving and national distribution of activity in this area is patchy at present. Improved data collection on a national basis will be developed by building on current initiatives, encouraging the development of collection methodologies, and seeking wider dissemination of information which will be of practical use at the local level.

33. In Scotland, the Scottish Centre for Infection and Environmental Health (SCIEH) acts as a source of expert advice on environmental health matters and coordinates surveillance activities. In Wales, the All Wales Environmental Health Surveillance Project has collated information on the public health consequences of acute chemical incidents over the past three years. The lessons from the 600 incidents reported are now being taken forward through the development of a Chemical Incident Management Support Unit, which will advise local and health authorities. Cardiff has also been chosen as the location of a WHO Collaborating Centre for the surveillance of major chemical incidents worldwide, commencing in July 1996. In Northern Ireland, this advisory and coordinating role is performed by the Department of Health and Social Security Services, Northern Ireland (DHSSNI).

34. Collection and analysis of **morbidity and mortality data**, which may indicate an association between public health and environmental factors, are being addressed in England in two, related, ways: the *Public Health Common Data Set (PHCDS)*[100]; and *Environmental Health Risk Indicators (EHRIs)*[44]. A PHCDS has been developed for Wales on the same principles (see para 41 below). The Information and Statistics Division of the Common Services Agency prepares the Scottish Key Indicators of Performance (SKIPPER) which contains information similar to the PHCDS.

35. The PHCDS is a comprehensive set of data on population health. It is designed and produced centrally *for use by the NHS in England* and contains a variety of health-related indicators, analysed by Health Authority area. The dataset was developed following a requirement by the DH that Health Authorities' Directors of Public Health should produce an annual report on the health of their resident populations. A joint working group of the DH and the Faculty of Public Health Medicine recommended central analysis of *available* data in order to avoid duplication of effort through each District having to do this separately. An added advantage of central analysis was the production of *comparative* data, which would not have been possible locally. DH is attempting to develop data relating to both health and the environment for the same geographical populations. Any correlations will need to allow for such factors as time lags and mobility of population.

36. Responsibility for the development and specification of the PHCDS rests with the Central Health Outcomes Unit within DH; responsibility for commissioning the analyses and publication of the dataset rests with the Department's Statistics Division.

37. DH has commissioned the University of Surrey to publish the PHCDS annually. It is distributed on magnetic disk, accompanied by an handbook[99], to Directors of Public Health in the NHS to supplement local data on the health of their populations. The University also produces a National Volume[100], in hard copy, which is available for sale. Analysis is at national, Regional (historically) and District Health Authority levels, and the handbook includes information on definitions and guidance on interpretation. There is a facility for health authorities (at their cost) to request local analyses at lower levels of aggregation.

38. The PHCDS has grown incrementally over five years and the set in 1994 incorporated indicators of progress against the national health targets for England set out in the Government's programme *The Health of the Nation*[65]. These targets address five key areas: cancers; coronary heart disease and stroke;

accidents; HIV/Aids and sexual health; and mental illness. An enforced delay in publication of the 1994 dataset was used by the PHCDS Steering Group as an opportunity to rationalise the dataset; to highlight and address any overlap and inconsistency between indicators; and to identify gaps for future development.

39. The PHCDS is dominated, especially at district level, by mortality data. Routine national datasets covering risk to health and morbidity are scant. Most current risk indicators are based on national surveys and may only be analysed at the level of NHS Regions. In recognition of this gap, a working group was set up to examine potential existing datasets from non-NHS sources, which might be used to develop new indicators, particularly on potential risk to health. Based on screening of datasets and topics, a few environmental topics were selected for further study.

40. This is a difficult area and as a first step (as an initiative in England, although the results may well be relevant elsewhere in the UK), the South-East Institute of Public Health was commissioned by DH to undertake feasibility studies of potential EHRIs, again using available data. The studies were required to:

- review evidence on the relationship between each risk factor and health;

- explore potential data sources;

- specify indicators suitable for the PHCDS; and

- comment on the extent to which the data might reflect local risk and be useful to Directors of Public Health in commenting on local health issues.

41. The Public Health Common Data Set for Wales (PHCDSW) was first published in 1989 to inform the Annual Reports for 1990 of the Directors of Public Medicine. Data were collected for 1983-1988 and mirrored the ten Health Gain Areas identified by the Welsh Health Planning Forum. The PHCDSW was later distributed to the nine Welsh Health Authorities. Currently the WO is funding the Acuity project which applies an Executive Information System to the PHCDSW. The PHCDSW concentrates heavily (as in England) on mortality data. Morbidity data relate to selected diagnosis and operational procedures.

42. On its own, formal surveillance of health hazards is unlikely to be totally adequate and will continue to rely on the alertness of clinicians and members of the public.

43 DoE will be investigating preferred methods of estimating exposure to noise as part of a comprehensive programme to quantify and assess noise problems and improve understanding of the

potential links between noise and health. Three contracts have been let at a cost of £270,000 in pursuit of these objectives.

Housing

44. Every five years the DoE conducts a house condition survey in England, which measures the state of repair, the extent of unfitness, the provision of facilities, dwelling size and energy efficiency of the housing stock. It also records the characteristics of the households occupying the dwellings, including information on long term illness and disability of household members. House condition surveys are also conducted in Northern Ireland, Scotland and Wales.

45. These surveys are powerful tools and represent a significant advantage in monitoring unfit housing. The quality and availability of health-related indoor and associated environmental data for the UK are further enhanced: by the collection of data on indoor air quality, including levels of radon, nitrous oxides, carbon monoxide, Volatile Organic Compounds (VOCs) and formaldehyde; by the collection of temperature and humidity data; by monitoring *Legionella sp* in water systems, particularly in cooling towers; and, by a programme of development designed to improve standards of fitness for dwelling houses. Issues which have been identified as the most important in the indoor environment include low temperatures, radon, environmental tobacco smoke, carbon monoxide and house dust mites. The issues addressed are regularly disseminated by publications, which include: *English House Conditions Survey 1991*[39], *The Scottish House Conditions Survey 1991*[117], *Building regulation and health*[15] , and *Building regulation and safety*[16].

46. Annual information on a more limited set of dwelling characteristics is also provided by the General Household Survey, which covers England, Scotland and Wales and by the Continuous Household Survey which covers Northern Ireland.

47. Local authorities are encouraged to undertake assessments of housing conditions in their areas in developing the housing strategies they submit annually to the DoE. Separate surveys are undertaken by some authorities of houses in multiple occupation. Local authorities also have quarterly returns on numbers of households in temporary accommodation having been accepted as homeless.

Occupational health

48. The HSE gathers occupational health data from several sources, including:

- reports by individuals responding to sample surveys of illness they attribute to work;

- records generated by statutory benefit and reporting systems;

- voluntary medical reporting schemes funded by the HSE; and

- deaths certified as due to disease likely to have been caused by work (for example, mesothelioma).

The data are used to indicate the magnitude of work-related ill health, monitor trends, help prioritise different hazards and identify particular problem areas. However, the data do not give a full picture and it is not possible to use them as performance indicators, because of the multi-factorial nature of some diseases, other factors influencing why people report illness or seek compensation, and the length of time between exposure to some workplace hazards and disease diagnosis.

Actions: Group 3

49. The following Group 3 actions are planned:

(1) In March 1996, the government published a preliminary set of *Indicators of Sustainable Development for the United Kingdom*[73]. As part of the ongoing process to consult on and improve upon the preliminary set of indicators, a seminar will be held in the summer of 1996 to canvas views from a wide range of users and contributors. An update of the Indicators is proposed by 1998.

(2) By summer 1996, DoE will complete its current study of the holding of information within DoE. Based on this, DoE will prepare a strategy to bring greater coherence to the gathering and holding of environmental information, to make information more readily accessible, and to help in the informing of policy and the monitoring of targets.

(3) DoE will continue to publish annually each April the *Digest*[32] (with summary statistics for Wales), including the same or comparative, updated information and developing the scope of coverage.

(4) In the second half of 1996, DoE will begin to produce an electronic core database based on information included in the *Digest*[32] as part of its contribution to the European Information and Observation Network (EIONET), being established by the EEA. DoE will make this database accessible through the World Wide Web of the Internet.

(5) The next edition of *The UK Environment* will be published in 1999.

(6) The Government will publish its response to the RCEP Report *Sustainable Use of Soils*[135] by the end of 1996.

(7) In December 1995, DH issued a consultation paper on proposals for the future development of the PHCDS; in mid 1996, based on that consultation, DH will decide the content and format of future datasets and to what extent to cross-link the PHCDS with other health service data sets.

(8) DH will further develop the EHRI.

(9) The Automated Urban Network will be expanded in 1996 to include a further ten centrally funded sites.

(10) By the end of 1996, DoE will integrate around 35 local authority automatic air quality monitoring sites into the national network, bringing the total number of sites to over 80.

(11) Greater recognition of the possible need for public health surveillance after a chemical contamination incident will be encouraged through more effective planning and response.

(12) By April 1996, DoE had let three contracts as part of a comprehensive programme to quantify and assess noise problems and improve understanding of the potential links between noise and health, at a cost of about £270 000. The results will be published during 1996 and 1997.

(13) The surveillance programmes will be maintained.

2.2 Assessment of Health-Related Environmental Hazards

Objectives

● To ensure that effective mechanisms exist for the identification and assessment of environmentally determined health hazards.

(EHAPE para 68)

Basis for action

Risk assessment

1. This section is concerned with mechanisms for the identification and assessment of risk in a broad sense. Action related to more specific areas is addressed in the relevant sections (for example, water in Section 3.1, air in Section 3.2).

2. Given the scientific knowledge available today, it is often possible to identify hazards to health - substances in the environment which are known to be toxic or microbiologically active. However, it may be much more difficult to distinguish those which will result in actual harm, or to assess and quantify the consequences for health which they present; and yet more difficult to evaluate the costs and benefits (not only monetary and not only to health) of removing or reducing that hazard, and the relative priority to be attached to that work. The effort to identify hazards, and to assess and quantify the risks they present, requires a multi-disciplinary approach. Similarly, a multi-disciplinary approach is required to the communication of information, to both the health professional and the wider public, about risk assessment and its implications.

3. Assessment of environmental hazards to health needs to be considered in two different sets of circumstances: the response to acute exposures, possibly at relatively high levels, for example following the accidental discharge of toxic substances to the environment; and surveillance of health effects of chronic exposures, often at very low levels. The actions required in both sets of circumstances are similar. In general terms, what is needed is:

> – to identify hazards present in the environment, and the levels at which they are present;
>
> – to quantify and assess the extent to which people are actually exposed, the route of exposure and the metabolic pathways by which that exposure may cause actual harm to health;

> – to take account of the multitude of other factors which may enhance or mitigate any effects on health (circumstances and level of exposure, interaction with other environmental factors, pre-existing clinical or socio-economic condition of those exposed, lifestyle, diet may all be relevant); and
>
> – to screen the resulting data using appropriate criteria and judgement to determine priorities and resource requirements for managing the identified environmental health risks.

There are close working relationships between Departments to achieve these objectives. Additionally, Departments consult experts within industry about assessments on individual substances. Appropriate Group 3 actions are set out in para 21 below.

4. A wide scale environmental risk evaluation in relation to health has been published[18] and applied for the buildings and indoor environment sector by the DoE's Executive Agency, the Building Research Establishment (BRE). The application of the BRE methodology allows the ranking of hazards to health by degree of severity in relation to buildings. These rankings are the most comprehensive produced to date for England and Wales, and cover a large number of data.

Responsibility for action

5. At the central Government level, responsibility for environmental issues in the UK and action upon them lie with a number of Government Departments all of which work closely together. The DH, in particular, works closely with other Departments whose responsibilities are relevant to public health.

6. In **England**, for the majority of non-occupational environmental risks to health, responsibility for action lies with DoE and MAFF; for microbiological safety of food and for communicable disease it lies with DH;

and for transport accidents, with Department of Transport (DOT).

7. In **Northern Ireland,** DoE(NI) has responsibility for action in relation to most non-occupational environmental risks to health and for transport accidents; DHSSNI for microbiological safety of food and communicable diseases, and also advises on the human health implications of policies.

8. In **Scotland and Wales**, for non occupational issues, responsibility for action rests with the SO and WO.

9. For **occupational health**, the HSC, working through the HSE, is responsible to Ministers. In July 1995, Ministerial responsibility for the HSC and HSE was transferred from the Department of Employment to the DoE.

10. There are also responsibilities at the local level. Local authorities have important and wide-ranging responsibilities for maintaining and improving the quality of the environment, including health-related aspects, in their areas. Health Authorities have responsibilities not only for the provision of primary and secondary health care but also for the wider public health and health promotion.

Scientific advice for Government policy-making

11. Government policy-making in the UK is informed by medical and scientific assessment of environmental hazards and the risks to health which they present. That assessment takes account of the available scientific evidence, whether commissioned by Government or published by other sources. There are a number of expert Advisory Committees the work of which is relevant to environment and health concerns: among the principal ones are:

– the Advisory Committees on Toxicity, Carcinogenicity and Mutagenicity of Chemicals in Food, Consumer Products and the Environment;

– the Advisory Committee on Pesticides;

– the Veterinary Products Committee;

– the Committee on Medical Aspects of Radiation in the Environment (COMARE);

– the Committee on the Medical Effects of Air Pollutants;

– the Advisory Committee on Microbiological Safety of Food;

– the Expert Panel on Air Quality Standards;

– the Quality of Urban Air Review Group;

– the Medical Research Council (MRC) Committee on Toxic Hazards in the Environment and Workplace;

– the MRC Committee on the Effects of Radiation;

– the Radioactive Waste Management Advisory Committee;

– the Advisory Committee on Hazardous Substances; and

– the Advisory Committee on Toxic Substances.

Advice on the effects of ionising and non-ionising radiation is provided by the NRPB.

12. The Advisory Committees provide an important and greatly valued source of advice from independent experts. Members of each Advisory Committee are selected on the basis of their individual expertise relevant to the work of the Committee, and may be employed in academia, the NHS, or industry; members are appointed, usually, for a renewable term of three to four years.

Surveillance of health effects of chemicals in the environment

13. The NHS, Government Departments and other organisations have responsibility for different aspects of public health effects of chemicals in the environment. At its most extreme this can mean responding to chemical accidents (See Section 3.6). On the every-day level it entails monitoring the possible health effects of 'routine' levels of chemicals in the environment.

14. Surveillance of health effects needs to be undertaken:

– at 'normal' levels of chemicals in the environment; and

– as longer term follow-up to the effects of chemical accidents.

In addition to providing information relevant to the provision of public health services, such surveillance of public health can also inform future decisions about environmental policy and its impact on public health.

15. The possible relationship between chemicals in the environment and human health is seldom clear cut. Scientific knowledge may be limited, for example: scientific evidence may relate to toxicity in animals which may be difficult to extrapolate to human beings;

evidence may be available only in relation to very high levels of exposure which the public are unlikely to encounter; and the mechanism by which a particular pollutant might affect human health may be unclear.

16. In considering and undertaking surveillance, it is important to recognise the need to prioritise the effort involved and to focus attention on those areas which are most likely to produce valid and useful information. It is unrealistic, and not cost-effective, to attempt to undertake monitoring and surveillance across too broad a spectrum.

17. Given the many scientific uncertainties about the human health effects of exposures to most chemicals and the many confounding factors which may influence health, it is difficult to provide comprehensive and flexible facilities which are effective and easily accessed by those who need to use them. DH is considering the best way forward, to ensure that appropriate support is available to those who need it to respond to chemical incidents or to monitor the health effects of 'routine' exposures to chemicals in the environment.

Small Areas Health Statistics Unit (SAHSU)

18. The incidence of disease in the UK at a local level is investigated by the SAHSU and a parallel unit at the ONS. SAHSU was established in 1987 to provide a centre of expertise for investigating alleged links between clusters of disease and industrial installations. Until the formation of SAHSU, there was no national facility for investigating health statistics in small geographical areas associated with point-source environmental pollution.

19. SAHSU holds a comprehensive database of postcoded cancer registry and mortality data. Using this database, SAHSU is capable of rapidly generating observed/expected rates of cancer incidence and mortality around any point source in Great Britain. In future, SAHSU will also have the capability to investigate cancer incidence and mortality around extended sources (for example, industrial complexes) and line sources (for example, roads, railway lines). The Unit also holds ONS data on live births, stillbirths, neonatal deaths and congenital malformations. The latter may present a particularly useful additional data set but there are currently considerable difficulties in its routine use because of the incomplete and variable quality of data from different areas of the country.

International activity

20. There is an extensive international effort to identify, assess and address environmental risks to health and the UK is an active contributor to these programmes. This includes the work of the WHO; Inter-Governmental Forum on Chemical Safety (IGFCS); International Programme on Chemical Safety (IPCS); Organisation for Economic Cooperation and Development (OECD); the European Science Foundation (ESF); the Council of Europe; and the EU work on risk assessment of new and existing substances.

Actions: Group 3

21. The following Group 3 actions are planned:

(1) The Government will maintain and further develop high quality scientific research initiatives for the identification and quantification of new or existing hazards to health, the levels to which the general public or vulnerable groups are exposed, and evaluation of associated risks to health. These include:

(i) routine collection, collation and evaluation of statistical data on morbidity and mortality at District, Regional and National levels;

(ii) routine collection, collation and evaluation of statistical data on occupational health (including the consequences of accidents);

(iii) research, including work by the SAHSU costing £600,000 over the next three years, into health status of populations close to point sources of pollution. The several reports will be published as they become available; and

(iv) further development and application of the health risk evaluation in the buildings and indoor environment sector, supported by improved data collection.

Further details of research are given in Section 2.8 of this plan.

(2) The Government will continue:

    (i)   to monitor and evaluate scientific evidence, obtained in this and other countries;

    (ii) to identify new or existing hazards to health, and levels of exposure;

    (iii) to assess the impact of such hazards, including those arising from proposed environmental development or change, upon the health of the general public or of vulnerable groups in the UK; and

    (iv) to ensure close cooperation and cohesion between Departments involved in assessing risks from chemical exposure in the workplace and environment.

(3) The Government will continue, and further develop, the UK's contribution to the international effort to identify, assess and address environmental risks to health.

(4) The Government will explore the most effective way of providing support to public health authorities in their response to chemical accidents and in the wider monitoring and surveillance of public health to detect possible adverse health effects of chemicals in the environment.

2.3 Control Measures

Objectives

- To develop an increasingly coherent and consistent body of agreements and regulatory instruments which include provisions for enforcement and review.

- To apply control measures to individual activities on the basis of objective assessments of hazards, without penalizing some activities unnecessarily.

(EHAPE para 102)

Basis for action

1. The control of environmental pollution is a fundamental contribution to improved health. This section divides consideration of the control of environmental pollution into two parts, dealing first with the control of outdoor and industrial pollution and then with the control of indoor pollution. Environmental health controls in relation to food are dealt with in Section 3.3; and in relation to occupational health and safety in Section 4.2.

2. In relation to the role of local authorities, it is the responsibility of Directors of Public Health (DPH) to work closely with local authorities to ensure that local authority and health authority plans and service provision are consistent, comprehensive and complementary, and that local authorities receive the health services input that they need to carry out their functions (see Section 2.5, para 11 on role and function of the DPH).

Outdoor and industrial pollution

General principles

3. As described in Chapter 1 (para 13), responsibility for the enforcement of outdoor and industrial pollution control lies with local authorities and, since 1 April 1996, with the EA, the Environment and Heritage Service, and the SEPA. The Agencies have become operational so recently that it is convenient in this section to describe their mode of operation in terms of their predecessor organisations: what is written about those predecessor organisations applies to their successors unless explicitly stated otherwise.

4. Over the last 30 years, environmental health in the UK has improved significantly owing to the adoption of environmental control measures: for example, measures to reduce exposure to lead in air, soil, water and food have contributed to a very substantial fall in blood lead levels. Sometimes improvements in the quality of releases were achieved by changing processes to avoid generating pollutants. However, separate legislation for the control of releases to different media was recognised as being inadequate because reductions in releases to one medium were often at the expense of increases in releases to another medium and, hence, did not represent an overall improvement in environmental quality.

5. The solution to this problem was the introduction of a system of Integrated Pollution Control (IPC) for industries with high pollution potential, in which the guiding principle was that the *best available techniques not entailing excessive cost* (BATNEEC) should be used to prevent releases or, where this was not practicable, to minimise and render harmless substances released. The philosophy behind BATNEEC is that an operator's expenditure to control pollution should be proportional to the environmental benefit it brings. BATNEEC should also be used to direct releases to the environmental medium best able to receive them, with the objective of minimising pollution of the environment as a whole. This is known as the Best Practicable Environmental Option (BPEO), which was the subject of the Twelfth Report of the RCEP[107].

6. Both BATNEEC and BPEO are site-specific in application, since the characteristics of site, geography and local environment will bear on both the costs and the benefits of pollution abatement and the practicability of particular options. Accordingly, in minimising the impact on environmental health, local conditions are brought into play within the framework of a nationally coordinated and regulated control procedure. However, Agency guidance is also produced on abatement techniques for each particular industrial sector, to lend transparency and consistency to the application of the concepts.

7. The UK has implemented a system of prior authorisation, in which operators apply for

authorisation, describing their process and evaluating BATNEEC and BPEO. In authorising the process, the regulator imposes legally enforceable conditions, for example on maximum release levels to environmental media at specific discharge points and the abatement techniques to be used. Authorisations also generally impose an improvement programme with a specified timetable within which the abatement techniques have to be upgraded.

8. The conditions are determined after statutory consultation with bodies which have an interest in environmental quality and with the general public. All concerns expressed must be considered in determining an application for authorisation. In some cases, conditions attached to authorisations may require the consideration of low level cumulative releases or ambient concentration monitoring. Conditions of authorisation are enforced by the imposition variously of enforcement or prohibition notices or, if required, by prosecution in the courts. If different conditions are required, for example as a result of either a process or a local environment change, they can be brought about by variation of the authorisation.

9. A separate system of Air Pollution Control (APC) operates in parallel to the IPC regime. It is concerned with industrial processes which have potential only to pollute air. Local authorities are responsible for the prior authorisation of such processes in England and Wales, whilst SEPA regulates them in Scotland. They operate under the same framework legislation as the IPC system, although since there is only potential to pollute one medium, there is no requirement for a BPEO assessment. There is the same principle of site-specific BATNEEC, here supported by guidance from the Secretary of State for the Environment. There is close liaison between those responsible for the IPC and APC regimes.

10. The regulations governing which processes are prescribed for control under IPC and APC are regularly reviewed and amended after a process of consultation. Regulated processes have their authorisations reviewed not less often than every four years to ensure that developments in abatement techniques and scientific knowledge are taken into account. International developments in Best Available Techniques are also kept under review, using independent research groups where necessary. Ongoing economic assessments are designed to ensure up to date BATNEEC assessment.

11. The UK monitors environmental quality standards for air and water and exceedance of these standards results in coordinated action. This may include temporary variations in permitted release levels from industrial processes, enforcement action, publicity, requests for voluntary restraint and so on, to achieve the standard.

Discharges to water

12. In considering authorisation of prescribed processes which involve discharges to water HMIP was required to consult the NRA (though both bodies are now part of the EA) a non-departmental public body created in 1989 to maintain and improve the water environment in England and Wales, as well as MAFF and the statutory consultees. In Scotland, this function was carried out by the RPAs. MAFF is responsible for assessing the potential impact on the human food chain of industrial emissions to air and of discharges to tidal waters. Comments on these emissions and discharges are taken into account in the final authorisation.

13. All the NRA's responsibilities have been inherited by the EA. These cover pollution control and water quality, water resources, fisheries, conservation, navigation and recreation. The EA also seeks to protect people and property against flooding by rivers and the sea. These powers and duties, including monitoring and enforcement, were exercisable in respect of inland freshwaters which includes rivers, lakes and canals (surface water) as well as underground waters (normally called groundwater), estuaries and coastal waters (the water quality and fisheries responsibilities being exercisable to three and six miles from the coast respectively). The EA is also responsible for enforcing certain European Commission (EC) Directives.

14. The EA is responsible for consenting discharges to water. The UK has long had a comprehensive set of informal water quality objectives which guide consenting and other pollution control activities by the EA. The Secretary of State announced in February 1995 that he intended to consult on statutory water quality objectives (SWQOs) on a trial basis in a small number of catchments in order to assess their effectiveness. The NRA prepared detailed proposals for SWQOs in eight pilot river catchments and the EA is now undertaking informal consultation on the proposals in order, among other things, to enable the costs and benefits to be assessed more precisely. There will then be formal consultation by the Government on the proposals. On the basis of these pilot studies, the Government will decide whether to proceed to an extended programme of SWQOs.

15. The main legislative provisions (certain parts of which are amended by the Environment Act 1995) for which the EA has inherited responsibility from the NRA are:

- Salmon and Freshwater Fisheries Act 1975;

- Water Resources Act 1991; and

- Land Drainage Act 1991.

16. The RPAs in Scotland performed broadly similar functions to the NRA. Those responsibilities have been inherited by the SEPA, whose responsibilities for controlled waters in its area (exercisable up to three miles from the coast) include water pollution control, monitoring of water quality, and the conservation of water resources so far as practicable. It also provides and operates flood warning systems. Like the EA, it has a general responsibility for consenting discharges to water.

17. The functions of SEPA are set out in the Environment Act 1995 which also modifies the main legislative provisions relating to discharges to water contained in:

- Rivers (Prevention of Pollution) (Scotland) Acts 1951 and 1965;

- Agriculture Act 1970;

- Control of Pollution Act 1974;

- Environmental Protection Act 1990; and

- Natural Heritage (Scotland) Act 1991.

18. In Northern Ireland, the Environment Service of DoENI was responsible under the Water Act (Northern Ireland) 1972 for the protection of the aquatic environment by preparing water quality management plans, monitoring water quality, controlling effluent discharges, and taking action to combat or minimise the effects of pollution.

19. The Agencies now have responsibilities in respect of certain EC Directives including:

- The Quality of Bathing Waters 76/160[172];

- The Dangerous Substances Directives 76/464[169], 83/513[161], 84/156[166], 84/491[163], 86/280[160], 88/347[164] and 90/415[162];

- The Freshwater Fish Directive 78/659[173];

- The Shellfish Waters Directive 79/923[174];

- Urban Waste Water Treatment Directive 91/271[177];

- Protection of waters against pollution caused by nitrates from agricultural sources Directive 91/676[171]; and

- The Standardised Reporting Directive 91/692[176].

20. In exercising its pollution control functions, the EA issues consents to water and sewerage companies for discharges from their water and sewage treatment works, and monitors the discharges for compliance with the terms of the consents. It performs an identical role for other industries that discharge effluent directly into rivers and other controlled waters.

21. In Scotland, the SEPA issues similar consents to water and sewage authorities and to industrial discharges. Consent conditions are designed to achieve Environmental Quality Standards (EQSs) for specific substances, which in turn enforce the Environmental Quality Objectives (EQOs) set out in EC Dangerous Substances Directives. Industrial discharges (including those containing *Red List Substances*) arising from prescribed processes (Part A processes) which were regulated by the HMIPI and RPAs are now regulated by SEPA.

22. In Northern Ireland, the Environment and Heritage Service has inherited the responsibility for controlling industrial and effluent discharges by means of a system of statutory consents under the Water Act (Northern Ireland) 1972.

Noise

23. The provisions of the Environmental Protection Act 1990 cover both proactive (anticipatory) and reactive (in response to complaint) nuisance control. Noise and vibration from many sources, including industrial processes, whether or not these processes are prescribed processes for IPC or local authority air pollution control (LAAPC), are controlled under this legislation. Other defined nuisances include any fumes or gases emitted from premises, together with any dust, steam, smell or other effluvia arising on industrial, trade or business premises and being prejudicial to health or a nuisance. Local authorities have powers to prevent or abate a statutory nuisance through the service of abatement notices. Those who breach abatement notices are liable to prosecution. There are fines of up to £5,000 for statutory nuisances on domestic premises and of up to £20,000 for industrial, trade or business premises. In court proceedings relating to industrial, trade or business premises, it would be a valid defence to show that the best practicable means of control had been used.

24. The Integrated Pollution Prevention and Control (IPPC) Directive proposes that control of noise and vibration be included in the prior authorisation of prescribed processes and a number of other industries.

I   A series of BREEAM reports is available from Construction Research Communications Ltd, 151 Rosebery Avenue, London, EC1R 4QX.

Other issues

25. Through BRE, the UK has taken an international lead in developing the BRE Environmental Assessment Method (BREEAM)[1], a voluntary scheme for minimising the impact of buildings on the indoor, local and global environment. Although primarily concerned with aspects of environmental quality that are not directly health related, BREEAM covers several issues that impact on environmental health, such as noise and indoor air quality. As well as the perceived benefit of improved workplace productivity, an additional health benefit of 'green' buildings, yet to be quantified, is the psychological well-being experienced by building occupants at ease with their physical environment.

26. Further control measures in relation to disasters are described in Section 3.6.

Indoor pollution

27. In England and Wales, both the Building Regulations and the Housing Fitness Standards, which cover new building work, have requirements for ventilation such that an adequate supply of air is provided for people in the building. Revised provisions which came into force in 1995 extend the requirements to non-domestic buildings and improve the performance in dwellings.

28. In Scotland, the Building Standards Regulations require ventilation of buildings to maintain adequate indoor air quality. This requirement has existed since 1964 and applies to almost all new buildings, and to those being substantially altered. (Only buildings covered by the Factories Act are currently exempt.) Since 1990, mechanical extract ventilation of kitchens and bathrooms in dwellings has been required to control humidity levels. There are also requirements, to ensure adequate combustion air for fuel burning appliances and for control of smoke created during a fire in the building, which are principally concerned with safety but may also improve indoor air quality.

29. Local authorities take the lead in controlling indoor air quality, using in England and Wales the general provisions of Part III of the Environmental Protection Act 1990 relating to matters which are prejudicial to health or a nuisance. In Scotland, Part II of the Public Health (Scotland) Act 1897, as amended, has similar provisions, as does the Public Health (Ireland) Act 1878, which covers Northern Ireland. Investigations carried out to assess conditions are generally at the instigation of the owner or tenant, and resolution may take the form of service of formal statutory notices which, if not complied with, result either in prosecution or remedial action in default of the owner or occupier directly by the local authority.

30. Indoor air pollution in the workplace is dealt with in Section 4.2.

Actions: Group 1

31. The following Group 1 actions are planned:

   (1) Local authorities will review and assess air quality in their areas and, where national air quality standards may not be achieved within the relevant period defined in the National Air Quality Strategy, will establish Air Quality Management Areas (AQMAs).

   (2) Within an AQMA, local authorities will prepare an action plan to improve local air quality and use their planning, transport and pollution control powers to help ensure air quality targets are met.

Actions: Group 2

32. The following Group 2 actions are planned:

   (1) Local authorities will develop local air quality management strategies to bring about long term improvements in local air quality.

Actions: Group 3

33. The following Group 3 actions are planned:

   (1) The Agencies will continue to review Best Available Techniques using independent research groups, making use of all technologies available worldwide.

   (2) At least at the four yearly review, but earlier if there is a significant change in BATNEEC, existing authorisations will continue to be reviewed and amended as required.

2.4 Economic and Fiscal Instruments

Objectives

- To improve the functioning of market and planning mechanisms in the private and public sectors, e.g. through economic incentives, so that they take account of health and environmental values and make prices reflect the full cost to society of production and consumption, including environmental health costs.

- To encourage, through financial incentives, investments in environmental health.

(EHAPE para 112)

Basis for action

1. In 1993 the DoE published the booklet *Making Markets Work for the Environment*[77]. That booklet explained how economic instruments can, in some cases, be a more flexible and cost effective way of achieving environmental objectives than direct regulation. Economic instruments include pollution taxes, product charges, tradeable emissions permits and deposit-refund schemes.

2. Economic instruments work by attaching a cost to making use of the environment. This ensures that individuals and firms take the full social costs of their actions into account when deciding what to consume or produce, and adjust their behaviour accordingly. The use of economic instruments to achieve environmental objectives is therefore in line with *the polluter pays principle*.

3. Economic instruments, direct regulation and voluntary action can be used separately or in combination in pursuing particular environmental policy objectives. Normally, an appropriate balance is found when economic instruments are used to encourage businesses and individuals to improve their environmental performance beyond the strict requirements of the law, regulation is used to prevent unacceptable damage to the environment, and encouragement of voluntary action to achieve still further improvements to environmental quality. The policy of encouraging motorists to use unleaded petrol is a case in point:

- the tax differential between leaded and unleaded petrol, though clearly important, was supported by a publicity campaign; and

- 'two star' petrol was phased out by amendments to regulations.

4. Transport is one policy area where economic instruments have a key role to play. For example, the environmental and health impacts of using various automotive fuels are taken into account when considering the level and structure of excise duties. In the 1994 Budget, the elimination of the differential (measured in pence per litre) in favour of diesel took account, among other things, of increased concern about the health effects of particulates from diesel engines. In the 1995 Budget, the Government renewed its commitment to increasing road fuel duty by 5% in real terms. The Chancellor also reduced the duty on road fuel gases by 15% in recognition that they are relatively cleaner fuels, and increased the tax on super-unleaded petrol by a further 4 pence per litre from May 1996 in view of the fact that its use in vehicles without catalytic converters can lead to higher emissions of pollutants such as benzene.

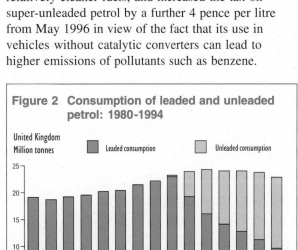

Figure 2 Consumption of leaded and unleaded petrol: 1980-1994

United Kingdom Million tonnes — Leaded consumption — Unleaded consumption

Thousand tonnes							
Lead emissions	1980	1985	1990	1991	1992	1993	1994
Petrol-engined road vehicles	7.5	6.5	2.2	2.0	1.7	1.5	1.3

Uptake of unleaded petrol increased from virtually zero in 1987 to nearly 60% of total UK petrol consumption by December 1994. This trend has been helped by the favourable fiscal treatment given to unleaded petrol to promote its use. Unleaded petrol is expected to account for 90% of all petrol sales by the end of the century. Emissions of lead from road vehicles have fallen by 83% since 1980, as a result of controls on the lead content of fuels and the introduction of unleaded petrol.

Source: NETCEN

5. Increased traffic congestion can also lead to a deterioration in the local environment by increasing air pollution and noise. One option for reducing congestion is to charge road users each time they make use of a road, to provide an incentive to cut down on unnecessary trips and ease the flow of traffic. However, feasibility studies of road pricing have identified a number of practical difficulties, which suggests that initial moves in this direction would need to be modest in scope.

6. In principle, an environmental health strategy should strike an appropriate balance between the costs and benefits from achieving reductions in pollution: in practice, it may be difficult to assess the precise risks to the environment and health if scientific evidence is not conclusive. Accordingly, it is Government policy to follow the precautionary principle, set out in *This Common Inheritance* [138]:

> "Where there are significant risk of damage to the environment, the Government will be prepared to take precautionary action to limit the use of potentially dangerous pollutants, even where scientific knowledge is not conclusive, if the balance of costs and benefits justifies it."

There are also problems in placing an economic value on any damage caused, although work is in hand in this area.

7. The DoE published the booklet *Policy Appraisal and the Environment: A Guide for Government Departments* [95] in 1991. The aim was to encourage a more effective integration of environmental concerns into Government policy assessments to ensure that decisions took full account of potential impacts on the environment. The guide, which was aimed primarily at economists, other specialists and policy-makers across a range of Government Departments, set out a broad appraisal framework and provided advice and guidance on a number of methodological issues. These included the identification of environmental impacts, and the role of valuation and other techniques such as weighting and scoring.

8. In 1994, the Government published a series of case studies in a booklet entitled *Environmental Appraisal in Government Departments* [40], which examined how environmental appraisal had been used in a range of policy analyses across Government Departments, including the DoE, DOT and MAFF. A project will shortly be let to evaluate the effect of *Policy Appraisal and the Environment* [95] on decision making in central Government.

9. There has been increasing interest in the development of environmental accounts which would provide some measure of environmental degradation and resource depletion. Such accounts are envisaged as 'satellite' or supplementary accounts which would leave the national accounts unchanged: this is because there are substantial conceptual and methodological difficulties in developing such environmental accounts. In 1994, the UK in association with other countries formed a group of national environmental/national accounting experts (the 'London Group') with the aim of developing environmental accounts linked to standard national accounting principles.

Actions: Group 3

10. The following Group 3 actions are planned:

   (1) The ONS unit developing a system of satellite accounts will compile a preliminary satellite account by summer 1996, one element of which will be air pollution. A more complete set of accounts will be available by summer 1997.

   (2) An evaluation of progress on environmental appraisal across government resulting from *Policy Appraisal and the Environment* [95] will be completed by the end of 1996.

   (3) A DoE sponsored study looking at the costs of acid rain (including health effects) will be published by Earthscan this summer (1996).

   (4) A landfill tax will be introduced later this year (1996).

2.5 Environmental Health Services

Objectives

- To develop at national, subnational and local levels appropriate environmental health services, and the necessary supporting mechanisms, to implement policies to control, prevent and correct environmental factors with adverse effects on health and, where appropriate, promote those which enhance human health and wellbeing.

(EHAPE para 121)

Basis for action

1. The foundations of environmental health management were laid over the course of the last 150 years or so. The towns and cities which had grown rapidly during the industrial revolution overwhelmed the limited services then available. In response, a significant infrastructure developed to provide and improve environmental health services for the changing needs of the population. As environmental health needs changed, so the professions established to deal with them also had to change, adapt, and develop to address the new or emerging problems.

2. Against this background of changing needs, central government had to set the overall policy and promulgate the legislation needed to enable organisational and operational changes to be implemented at local level. This has resulted in a framework where objectives and legislation are set nationally by central government departments, whilst the environmental health services are operated mainly at the community level through local government units. The history of these developments has been briefly described in the introduction to the Audit Commission's *Towards a Healthier Environment*[140].

Central government departments

3. There is no single government department responsible for the whole environmental health function: UK Health Departments have responsibilities within central government for health related aspects of environmental health; and Environment Departments for the environmental aspects. The division of responsibilities between government departments and between central government and local authorities is shown in Annex 5.

4. Annex 5 also describes the role of Environmental Health Officers (EHOs) and shows that environmental health is affected by a great variety of factors ranging from planning to epidemiological surveillance.

Locally, each factor will vary both in absolute terms and in the importance attached to it by the public. Moreover, there may be synergistic effects with other factors. A holistic local approach is therefore essential if an effective environmental health service is to be achieved.

5. The White Paper, *The Health of the Nation*[65], set the overall goal of securing continuing improvement in the general health of the population of England by:

- adding years to life: an increase in life expectancy and reduction in premature death; and

- adding life to years: increasing years lived free from ill health, reducing or minimising the adverse effects of illness and disability, promoting healthy lifestyles, physical and social environments and overall, improving quality of life.

6. The *Health of the Nation* (HON) initiative represents a major step forward as the first long term strategy aiming to improve the health of the people in England. Similar policy statements have been published in Northern Ireland, Scotland and Wales with targets which reflected the health priorities of those countries. The relevant documents are:

A Regional Strategy for the Northern Ireland Health and Personal Social Services 1992-1997.[109]

Health Education in Scotland – a National Policy Statement.[62]

Scotland's Health – A Challenge to us All.[116]

Strategic Intent and Direction for the NHS in Wales.[130]

7. The documents recognise the important and diverse roles that many people and organisations have to play,

particularly through working together in active partnerships to improve health in what are known as healthy alliances. Local authorities have a major impact on the health of the community and their importance is recognised. The documents identify and represent a new way of working. Success of the strategy will come through:

> - public policies – policy makers at all levels considering the health dimension when developing policies (Guidance[96] was published in December 1995);
>
> - healthy surroundings – active promotion at home, at work and at large of physical environments conducive to health;
>
> - healthy lifestyles – through increased public awareness as to how lifestyles can affect health; and
>
> - high quality health services – by identifying and meeting the health needs of local populations, by researching and monitoring, which will determine the most effective ways of improving health.

8. These strategies highlight the importance of healthy alliances. Many such alliances have been established in response to the HON initiative. The DH encourages this and spreads good practice developed by existing alliances, through its Health Alliance Awards Scheme. Details of the 24 alliances shortlisted for the 1995 national Awards can be found in *Fit for the Future*[52], the second progress report on the HON.

9. There is a need to strike the right balance between enforcement and education. New legislation in many areas has of necessity addressed this relationship, and the Government's deregulation initiative has been a key focus in this area. Partnership can often advance environmental health issues more effectively than enforcement for two reasons: firstly, enforcement is often to ensure a minimum standard, whereas partnership may lead to agreement on a better than minimum standard; and secondly, partnership may often bring benefits of synergy. However, in fairness to those who accept their responsibilities, enforcement may be necessary to deal with those who would seek to avoid them.

Public health in the National Health Service

10. Within the NHS, departments of public health ensure that public health considerations – including those associated with environmental factors – are fully taken into account in arrangements for the promotion and delivery of health-care in their areas.

11. At the Regional level, within the NHS Executive, DPH responsibilities include:

- public health input to central policy and strategy development;

- ensuring delivery of national public health support functions, including outcomes assessment, cancer registries, and national confidential enquiries;

- ensuring provision of support for NHS activity in the control of communicable disease and non-communicable environmental exposures;

- ensuring implementation of public health initiatives, such as the HON, within and through the NHS;

- performance management of public health functions and systems, in and between health authorities;

- ensuring that health authorities have access to adequate and appropriate support for their public health functions, including appropriate access to DH expertise and resources; and

- commissioning of research and development to support the above.

12. At the District level, DPH responsibilities include:

- assessing local health needs;

- developing and, as appropriate, implementing, local health and health promotion strategies;

- leading the health authority's work in improving the appropriateness and effectiveness of clinical and non-clinical interventions;

- a key role in developing and sustaining relationships between the health authority and clinicians (including general practitioners), local authorities and the local community;

- surveillance, monitoring and control of communicable disease and non-communicable environmental exposures in the district, in collaboration with local authorities and other agencies; and

- providing the focus for public health advice and information in their areas.

Environmental awareness and reporting

13. Within the last 5 years, environmental activity at local government level has increased considerably. This has reflected the general public's growing awareness of environmental and public health issues, which has been fuelled by the realisation of the

importance of safeguarding the environment. The World Conference on Environment and Development in Rio de Janeiro in 1992 gave momentum to the promotion of Local Agenda 21 processes within local authorities, enabling the principles behind sustainable development to flourish at a local level. The importance of the inter-sectoral approach, and partnership are among the fundamental principles. The cooperation between all key professionals in local authorities is a major factor in the implementation of policies that take account of both the short-term needs of the community and the long-term global needs.

14. State of the environment reporting is becoming an increasingly vital tool in the collection of statistical and other information relating to the health and needs of the population. While this concept is in itself not new, the principle has been extended to cover a broader picture of the local scene. The reports can be used for setting targets, for monitoring progress and for judging the success or otherwise of the strategies adopted. In 1995, *Indicators for Local Agenda 21*[72] was published, reporting the experience of ten pilot local authorities that worked with their local communities to agree sets of local sustainability indicators.

15. The UK recognises that much environmental policy is driven at international level (Codex, WHO, etc) and supra-regional level (European Community), which requires inter-sectoral collaboration on a much wider scale.

16. Partnerships make the enforcer's job easier, enable local authorities to attain the wider objectives on environmental health issues, and provide the means to fulfil the needs of the local community. Government has encouraged these partnerships, because, without the support of local people and business, it will become increasingly difficult to implement improvements in environmental health and to achieve the objectives of sustainable development. Accordingly, as part of the implementation of the HON strategy, the DH has published *Working Together for Better Health*[151] as guidance on alliance working; has established the Health Alliance Awards Scheme to reward and publicise successful and innovative alliance working; and is setting up a two-year project to establish alliances for workplace health promotion.

Target setting and monitoring of performance

17. Within the UK, central government has set targets for achievement and set in place mechanisms for monitoring. In **England**, *The Health of the Nation*[65] set 5 target areas for action to reduce: coronary heart disease and stroke; cancers; mental illness; HIV/AIDS and sexual health; and accidents. The targets for **Scotland** are to reduce premature deaths from coronary heart disease and cancers; to lower smoking prevalence and alcohol misuse; and to improve dental health. In **Northern Ireland and Wales**, targets have been set to reflect the local health priorities. In all four countries, improvements in environmental health services contribute to the achievement of the overall aims of their strategies.

18. Target setting and performance monitoring relies on the environmental services providing raw data which can be used for essential information and for policy decisions. To this end there will continue to be support for a wide network of information gathering of data at local and national level:

(i) for microbiology, the Communicable Disease Surveillance Centres of the PHLS are centres of excellence in England and Wales for the collection and analysis of local data. The aim of the PHLS is to improve the health of the population through the diagnosis, prevention and control of infections and communicable diseases in England and Wales. Parallel arrangements exist in Scotland.

(ii) Central government departments also require local authorities to provide data returns to inform policy decisions. Returns relating to housing conditions, inspections of food premises, samples of food taken for analysis, accidents at work, accidents in the home, morbidity and mortality data are used to assess which environmental health services meet present needs and to set targets for future requirements. In Northern Ireland, the 26 district councils are required to prepare Environmental Health Plans setting out a programme of action for their areas.

(iii) whilst local authorities are independent of central government, in many areas mechanisms exist to ensure that national policies can be implemented effectively at local levels. For food safety, local authorities have responsibility in the formulation and setting of their service levels, for achieving standards which have been set in statutory codes of practice. In many areas targets are set using a risk related approach, with the highest risk activities receiving the most attention.

(iv) local authorities, as local service providers, are close enough to the public and the industries which they serve to be able to identify and recognise local problems and to categorise those problems for action and control. Work is coordinated both at local level and at national level with multi-disciplinary and multi-sectoral agencies coming together to address their respective problems and priorities. Close working arrangements exist between the NHS and local authorities and, where enforcement is undertaken directly at central government level, government departments.

Appraisal of health

19. In accordance with a commitment in *Health of the Nation*[65] to produce guidance on the appraisal of health, including environmental health, a document *Policy Appraisal and Health*[96] was published in December 1995. It has been circulated widely throughout local and central government, the NHS and academic institutions and it has attracted widespread interest.

Actions: Group 2

20. The following Group 2 actions are proposed:

(1) The Government will continue to set out formally the aims and priorities for improving health through the Health of the Nation (HON) initiative and similar policy statements for Scotland, Wales and Northern Ireland.

(2) Local authorities will individually assess and prepare similar proposals, with targets and supplementary indicators, to meet local needs, having regard to the agenda set by central government.

2.6 Professional Training and Education

Objectives

- To provide education and training at all levels so as to create cadres and teams of environmental health professionals who will be responsible for implementing and managing specific programmes to improve environmental health.

(EHAPE para 129)

Basis for action

A framework for the profession

1. Environmental health is a multifaceted subject; it embraces biology, engineering, science and social interaction. Accordingly, practitioners in this field include such diverse professionals as environmental engineers and scientists, Environmental Health Officers (EHOs), epidemiologists, food and occupational hygienists, health promotion professionals, nurses, physicians, pollution control specialists, public health engineers and veterinarians.

2. Many of the professionals concerned with improving health and the environment work in the public and private environmental health sectors. However, a further large but disparate number work in health promotion and public health educational bodies. Accordingly, the two principal elements affecting education and training of environmental health professionals are:

(i) that directed towards present and future enforcement officers and intended to place in a sound scientific context their work in enforcing legislation and encouraging good practice; and

(ii) that directed more broadly within medical, scientific and engineering communities and closely associated with research relevant to the maintenance and improvement of environmental standards.

The prospects for improved controls and standards for the environment and health depend upon coordinated action, adequate training and sufficient numbers of people.

The key organisations

3. The organisations which play the most significant roles include:

- the Chartered Institute for Environmental Health;
- the Health Education Authority (HEA);
- the Health Education Board for Scotland;
- the Health Visitors Association;
- the Royal College of Physicians' Faculties of Public Health Medicine and Occupational Medicine;
- the Royal Environmental Health Institute of Scotland;
- the Royal Institute of Public Health and Hygiene (RIPHH);
- the Royal Society for the Promotion of Health (RSH);
- the Society of Health Education and Health Promotion Specialists (SHEPS); and
- university departments of public and environmental health.

4. Other representative bodies which carry out educational programmes covering their own specialists areas include:

- the Chartered Institution of Water and Environmental Management;
- the Environmental Services Association;
- the Institute of Waste Management;
- Water Training International; and
- many trade and employing organisations.

5. The bodies concerned with environmental management and enforcement are described in Section 2.5 and Annex 5.

A multi-faceted profession

6. The success of policies to enhance health and the environment depends upon a harmonious and effective inter-disciplinary collaboration. There is a need, therefore, for a network which facilitates exchange of information, encourages mutually supportive actions of the organizations concerned, and allows ready interpretation and evaluation of their activities. At senior levels, practitioners must be able to take an holistic view.

7. One of the basic principles of environmental health is the concept of dealing with problems 'at source' rather than 'at end of pipe'. Industry and the private sector are increasingly applying this principle. Environmental managers are already employed within the private sector in the UK; however, by developing educational and training programmes as an integrated part of other business disciplines, awareness of environmental health considerations can be incorporated from an early stage.

8. Because the UK has a long standing and well-developed infrastructure for environmental health personnel, there is a diverse range of career structures. Some are based on vocational training in particular areas of environmental services, and others on full graduate and postgraduate qualifications. Access to training is available through the many bodies mentioned in paras 3 and 4 above and through short courses provided directly by Government Departments. The challenge is to ensure that existing and future environmental health professionals are able to respond and adapt to the changing needs and desires of industry, government and society. Training and continuing development of skills are a significant part of the service's professionalism.

9. There will continue to be a need:

- to coordinate professional environmental health education and training programmes in order to ensure the maintenance of an intersectoral approach to the provision of environmental health services;

- to assess appropriate professional profiles to deliver effective environmental health services. Such assessment can aid the development of the core skills required by environmental health professionals and could make a significant contribution to the WHO/EURO project on environmental health staffing education and training which is currently at its developmental stage;

- to stress the interdisciplinary nature of environmental health and of the roles and functions of the various environmental health professionals;

- to develop the holistic and intersectoral approach; and

- to strengthen the partnerships between the employers of environmental health professionals and the training establishments, through sponsorship and co-funding arrangements. This can ensure that the provision of environmental health professional training is market led.

10. Such analysis of future educational and training needs is common to any profession and the self-motivated nature of the parties involved can be relied upon to ensure that the needs are met. Thus, for instance, the Welsh Combined Centres for Public Health have a role in coordinating professional environmental health education and training programmes; and, in addition, the Welsh Collaboration for Health and the Environment is a grouping of the Chief Environmental Health Officers, Directors of Public Health and Consultants in Communicable Disease Control, which has the objective of improving health in Wales through collaboration between those working in the public health area.

Actions: Group 3

11. No specific actions are planned.

2.7 Public Information and Health Education

Objectives

- To ensure and enhance participation of the public at the earliest stage in environmental health planning, priority-setting and programme implementation. Such involvement should be based on the principle of openness and equal partnership of all involved.

- To foster such active participation by the public, the necessary knowledge of the environment and health should be ensured, through effective health education programmes and the development of easily accessible information sources.

(EHAPE para 139)

Basis for action

Environment and health information

1. Any person has a statutory right under regulations[45] to request environmental information held by a wide range of public authorities and other bodies in Great Britain. The regulations implement *European Commission, EC Directive 90/313*[155] on the freedom of access to information on the environment. The regulations place a duty on bodies to make available information, subject to various discretionary or mandatory exemptions covering, for example, commercial confidentiality and personal information.

2. A person's rights under the regulations are additional to their other rights to inspect the many different types of statutory registers of environmental information covering, for example, authorisations under pollution control regulatory systems.

3. In April 1994, the *Code of Practice on Access to Government Information*[21] was introduced. The Code aims to promote informed policy making and debate and efficient service delivery. It also aims to provide timely and accessible information to the public. It restricts access to information only where there are good reasons for doing so. The EA is planning to make information available through the Internet, and is currently preparing its Code of Openness to ensure that environmental information is disseminated widely. The EA is responsible for collating environmental information and its research work is widely publicised, often with copies being placed in local libraries.

Government policy initiatives

4. A guide to *Policy Appraisal and the Environment*[95] was published in 1991. It is designed to increase awareness across government of the need to examine systematically the effects on the environment of existing and proposed policies. A further booklet[40] was published in 1994 giving details of environmental appraisal case studies and general guidance produced by various Government Departments. A 1994 evaluation of experience with the 1991 guide showed that in some cases it had had an impact on the development of policies.

5. In January 1995, the Prime Minister launched the UK Sustainable Development Strategy. One of the initiatives he announced was the *Going for Green* campaign.

Going for Green

6. *Going for Green* exists to promote messages of sustainable development to the general public. It aims to inform and motivate individuals to make changes to their lifestyles which will, taken together, make a difference to the environment and hence to people's health. In February 1995, the national committee, launched its campaign:

- to reduce earth, air and water pollution;
- to create, protect and improve local environments; and
- to reduce demands on precious resources.

7. The campaign will work in five main ways:

(i) by combining environmental initiatives to maximise their impact;

(ii) by establishing realistic goals, and a system to measure how effective they are; and

(iii) by encouraging individuals to "think green" in their daily lives. A major public awareness campaign was launched in February 1996, with a new national *Green Code* to help the public follow a more environmentally-sustainable lifestyle.

(iv) by using the media, to reach people in all walks of life, and seeking to influence those in positions of responsibility to help others to be 'greener'; and

(v) by 'Sustainable Communities' Pilot Projects (in Lancashire, Sedgefield, Huntingdonshire, Merton, and one each in Wales and Northern Ireland) to examine the practicality of the lifestyle changes that *Going for Green* suggests, by testing the ideas out in small well-defined communities. A related pilot project is being set up in Scotland as a partnership between *Going for Green* and *Forward Scotland*.

Education

8. Schoolchildren aged 5 to 16 are educated about the environment chiefly through the geography, science and technology curricula. Science teaching also contains aspects of health education. The Government encourages schools to support provision in the National Curriculum on preventative health issues, such as food hygiene, through their programmes of personal, social and health education. Within the statutory framework for such provision it remains, however, for individual schools to determine how best to organise and deliver the curriculum to meet their pupils' needs and to consider whether and, if so, how they wish to extend provision for education about preventative health issues, such as food hygiene, beyond this.

9. The Government has promised a five year moratorium until the year 2000 on further change to the National Curriculum, offering an opportunity to undertake a systematic evaluation of its content and structure. The School Curriculum and Assessment Authority (SCAA) is responsible for advising the Government on the school curriculum. As part of its Monitoring Programme, SCAA will ensure that there is sound evidence available to enable the Secretary of State to make decisions about whether further improvements are required and if so what those improvements should be.

10. A committee appointed to review the state of environmental education in further and higher education in England and Wales, and to recommend priorities for its future development, issued a report[47]

in 1993 (the 'Toyne Report'). The committee considered the whole range of environmental education provision, including courses to educate and train environmental and other relevant specialised personnel. Most of the report's recommendations concerned further and higher education institutions. It also made recommendations concerning the provision of continuing professional education for those already in the workforce. The Government sent colleges and universities copies of the Report, drawing their attention to its recommendations. Professor Toyne has been commissioned to undertake a survey of developments since 1993.

11. In Scotland, the Report *Learning for Life*[76] from the Working Group on Environmental Education made over 90 recommendations for action by a wide range of organisations. The Report set out a strategy for environmental education for the next ten years and it received overwhelming public support. The Secretary of State for Scotland published *A Scottish Strategy for Environmental Education*[118], which commends the original Report as a strong foundation on which developments in Scottish environmental education policy will be based. The Secretary of State's own Advisory Group on Sustainable Development has agreed to play a central role in the development of environmental education in Scotland and has set up the Education for Sustainable Development Group.

Health promotion

12. The HEA is the statutory body responsible for health education in England and carries out public education health campaigns such as the *Sun Know How* campaign. The HEA also coordinates the UK arm of the European Network of Health Promoting Schools initiative which aims to develop and assess the effectiveness of school-based health education strategies in changing and shaping pupils' behaviour. In Wales, Health Promotion Wales has responsibility for undertaking national campaigns.

13. In England from 1996/97, national health promotion work will be awarded on the basis of competitive tender and the Government will choose the contractor best able to provide campaigns in particular areas. This will ensure that health promotion funds are spent effectively. Reducing teenage smoking continues to be a priority and a competitive tender has been carried out to identify the best provider to develop this in 1996/97.

14. In Scotland, the Health Education Board for Scotland (HEBS) is the national centre for health education expertise and information. It undertakes health education programmes and gives a lead to the

health education effort in Scotland. This is achieved through liaison, coordination and close collaboration with other UK, Scottish and local bodies involved in health education. HEBS' programme, focus on the key health priorities identified in the Scottish national policy statement which are coronary heart disease, cancer, substance abuse (smoking, alcohol and drugs), physical activity, diet, accidents, dental and oral health, and HIV/AIDS.

15. To ensure that health promotion funds are used effectively in future, DH is funding research into the effectiveness of health promotion services. The intention behind this work is to ensure that health promotion methods of proven validity are employed in the future.

Leaflets

16. Government Departments and Agencies provide free information leaflets for the general public on many aspects of their responsibility which bear on environmental health. For example, DoE issues leaflets on such topics as air quality in the home, asbestos in housing, control of weeds on non-agricultural land, damp and mould in homes, house-dust mites, lead in paint, noise, reporting smoky diesel vehicles, smoking in public places, winter and summertime smog, and wood preservatives.

Risk communication

17. Some people's concerns about health and environmental risks have resulted in expenditure which has been out of all proportion to the benefit achieved. Since resources are inevitably limited, it is clearly wasteful to spend money in one area which would have greater benefit in another. This is a problem of risk communication which Government Departments are increasingly addressing through such publications as *A Guide to Risk Assessment and Risk Management for Environmental Protection*[61].

Action: Group 3

17. The following Group 3 actions are planned:

(1) The Government will provide information and advice to vulnerable groups regarding the most important environmental risks to health and the action that can be taken to remove or reduce these risks.

(2) The Government will establish a national air quality archive, available to the public on the Internet, by the end of 1996.

2.8 Research and Technological Development

Objectives

- To provide the scientific basis for policies aimed at identifying environmental hazards, assessing risks and reducing or preventing environmental effects on health.

- To provide appropriate technology and other tools for the maintenance and development of an environment that is conducive to health and wellbeing.

(EHAPE para 147)

Basis for action

The need for research and technological development

1. The UK agrees with the WHO that rational management of the environment in relation to health is often hampered by gaps in our knowledge of how the environment affects health. Among the specific gaps in our knowledge are:

> - how environmental factors relate quantitatively to health effects;
>
> - which population subgroups (defined by, for example, age, sex, genetic predisposition, sensitivity, nutritional conditions, pre-existing diseases) are more vulnerable to particular environmental factors and to what extent; and
>
> - the effect of multiple environmental factors that may interact with each other and with other factors (for example, lifestyles, socioeconomic factors), which themselves may contribute to the causation of the same diseases.

These gaps can be filled only through well planned and systematic research, which will often have an epidemiological element.

2. Such research should aim at defining indicators of exposure (which is almost always unknown for an individual) and/or early damage due to environmental agents at molecular, cellular and functional levels through laboratory investigations, and in populations using appropriate epidemiological studies. The Research Councils, in particular the MRC, through the Office of Science and Technology play a key role here in supporting research, with major relevant

investments by the MRC in its Applied Psychology, Medical Sociology, Toxicology, Radiobiology, Environmental Epidemiology, Reproductive Biology and Dunn Nutrition Units, and in the Centre for Mechanisms of Human Toxicology.

3. Environmental health management involves much more than mere recognition of the need to prevent or mitigate adverse environmental effects on health. Accordingly, research should also encompass the technological and economic fields, in order to develop technologies that are friendly to environmental health, and to reveal the extent to which their likely higher costs, compared with traditional technologies, are offset by net gains in health and wellbeing expressed in monetary terms. As an example, measures such as combined heat and power (CHP) schemes offer major financial gains to users, even when the costs of installing new technologies are considered. The use of CHP in hospitals has been encouraged by Health Departments and Environment Departments: there are some 200 CHP sets in operation in the NHS ranging in capacity from 38kW to 4.2MW. The Energy Efficiency Office and NHS Estates have both published guidance[8] on the use of CHP.

A strategy for research and technological development

4. The MRC's strategy on environment and health issues is being developed as part of the UK's national research effort. Its aims complement those of the other Research Councils, the Health Departments, the DoE, the Overseas Development Administration and Agencies. In 1993, the MRC, with the support of DoE and the DH, established the Institute for Environment and Health (IEH). The mission statement of the IEH is:

> "The Institute for Environment and Health will promote a healthier environment by facilitating information exchange, identifying and evaluating environmental health issues and managing research programmes on the adverse effects of chemicals, leading to a better understanding of the risks to human health and the environment from exposure to hazardous substances in air, water and soil."

A copy of the IEH's first report, *Air Pollution and Health: Understanding the Uncertainties*[6], was given to all delegations to the Helsinki Conference.

5. In 1995 the Government announced that, if sufficient projects of high quality are submitted, funding of up to about £5 million will be available in total for the UK in the period up to 1999 for the investigation of the effect of air pollution on respiratory disease. The IEH will act as manager for the allocation of the funds.

6. In 1993, the Government established a **Technology Foresight Programme** to help business people, engineers and scientists become better informed about each others efforts and to identify emerging opportunities in markets and technologies. Separate Panels were established to examine Health and Life Sciences, and Agriculture, Natural Resources and Environment. The Panels reported in 1995. The Health and Life Sciences Panel recognised the growing awareness and imminence of global environmental problems, which will lead to increasingly tough action from governments to reduce the consumption of energy and materials. The Agriculture, Natural Resources and Environment Panel called for the development of cleaner technologies as a response to pollution, and a reduction in the transmission of pollutants from the environment into the food chain and better screening of compounds prior to manufacture and release.

7. The DH's **Science and Technology Mission** is to maximise the benefits for health of its science and technology, and to apply rigorous research to the problems confronting the NHS, public health and the social services. Its research strategy comprises two complementary programmes, one centrally commissioned and the other the responsibility of the NHS, with an estimated total expenditure in 1995-6 of £69 million.

8. The UK also intends to investigate what interventions might prevent or ameliorate ill health where environmental factors are implicated, what public health advice could be offered to achieve these aims, and the most effective mode and delivery of that service.

Some specific concerns

9. A noise research advisory committee, comprising representatives of Government Departments and experienced noise researchers, is considering what more can be done to examine and understand the effects, including health risks, of exposure to noise. This issue forms part of the new DoE noise research programme. Future research will take account of and build upon the findings of earlier studies in the UK and elsewhere.

10. A relatively recent concern to emerge is the potentially disruptive effects on human and animal reproductive physiology of a number of man-made substances. Among such potential endocrine disruptors are oestrogenic substances including some pesticides, detergents, plasticisers and industrial chemicals such as some PCBs and dioxins. Specific research contracts have been let to investigate the problem (para 14 below).

11. Through the BRE, DoE carries out research into the health and safety of people in and around buildings. At the present time this programme includes:

- major reviews of health[15] and safety[16] in relation to the indoor environment and building features in the context of the Building Regulations and the Housing Fitness Standard;

- monitoring of the levels and sources of air pollutants in homes, including radon, formaldehyde, VOCs such as benzene, nitrogen dioxide, carbon monoxide, bacteria and fungi;

- means of preventing or reducing indoor air pollution, including source control (eg prevention of radon entry into homes) and ventilation by both mechanical and natural means;

- the causes and cures of sick building syndrome;

- the causes and consequences of damp homes (including colonisation by house dust mites) and how to reduce such problems;

- monitoring of dwelling stock condition and the costs of improvement;

- prevention of landfill gas transport and entry into buildings or spaces below buildings;

- health and safety, and energy implications of water supply systems;

- effects of low flows in drainage systems;

- safety of water heating appliances;

- prevention of contamination of drinking water;

- means of storage and collection of solid waste, including recycling;

- hygienic transport of wastewater from buildings;

- legionella related to water supply systems;

- avoidance of noise nuisance by physical improvements to dwellings and social means of reducing noise generation;

- a review of sources and levels of asbestos and man-made mineral fibres in and around housing;

- means of reducing emissions of carbon dioxide due to energy use[7]; and

- means of reducing emissions from ozone-depleting substances by improvement of methods for leak detection and assessment of performance of alternative refrigerants[59, 74].

12. The programme now managed by the EA includes scientific research and technological development to improve understanding of waste management processes, leading to better control; life cycle analysis to identify preferred options in environmental and economic terms for specific waste steams; improved capture of statistics about waste flows; and assessments of the efficacy of regulatory action, market based instruments and public awareness campaigns towards achieving the objectives set out in the National Waste Strategy. The results are disseminated both through research reports and through guidance documents. The joint DoE/ Department of Trade and Industry (DTI) Environmental Technology Best Practice Programme is aimed at improving the environmental performance, including waste minimisation, of selected industries by use of demonstration projects.

13. Additionally, there will continue to be non-Government research funded by a variety of sources including industry, charities etc, some of which will fund local research activity. The usual mechanisms of conferences, publications in peer reviewed journals etc allow the communication of important contributions to the field from such local research activities.

Actions: Group 2

14. The Government will promote research contracts.

(1) To identify environmental health indicators.

(2) To develop or improve methods for hazard identification and risk assessment.

(3) To determine quantitative dose-response relationships between exposures to recognised environmental hazards to health and health effects.

(4) To assess the risks of low-level and complex environmental exposures and of the effects on health of interactions between socioeconomic and lifestyle factors and environmental agents.

(5) To identify groups particularly vulnerable to exposure to certain environmental hazards.

(6) To identify damage-causing mechanisms in the general population and in vulnerable groups.

15. Reflecting current priorities in the UK, initiatives have already been established:

(1) To investigate endocrine disruptors including examination of the range of chemicals involved, development of appropriate testing methods, examination of foodstuffs and raw sewerage and drinking water for their presence, examination of effects of human populations and wildlife. A number of different Government Departments and agencies are involved in funding this work. Reports will begin to be available from Summer 1996 onwards.

(2) To investigate the effect of air pollution on respiratory disease.

(3) To improve methods of exposure measurement and modelling to give a realistic picture of the actual exposure of selected individuals and populations, and identify molecular, cellular and functional markers of early effects. A workshop was held at the IEH in December 1995 reviewing Biomarkers for Exposure, the report of this workshop is expected to be published before summer 1996.

(4) To sponsor and encourage research and development into options for waste minimisation, re-use and recycling, and environmentally sound disposal.

(5) To provide low-cost methods of monitoring food and air quality.

(6) To develop methods for comparing the costs of preventive action achieved through technological advances and other means and the gains expected in terms of health protection and promotion; also for comparing the detriments and benefits to health that the same economic activity may simultaneously bring about.

(7) To advance understanding of host-pathogen interactions in crop plants and farmed animals to underpin the development of new pest and disease control strategies which pose minimum risks to human health and the environment.

(8) To develop methods for the rapid analysis of trace quantities of molecules of biological relevance, both in the bioprocessing industry and in the environment for health and safety reasons and as quality assurance for therapeutic and other agents.

(9) To underpin the development of rational techniques for the safe design and operation of bioprocesses including new quantitative approaches to the risk appraisal for exposure to biological entities.

(10) To develop the science necessary to control microbial hazards and improve hygiene throughout the food chain from the raw material to the finished product.

(11) To consider what more can be done to examine and understand the effects, including health risks, of exposure to noise.

(12) To investigate the effects of ultra-violet radiation on skin cancer. Work is expected to be commissioned in 1996/97 and is expected to take 3-5 years.

(13) To investigate public perception of risk and develop improved methods of risk communication. An initial programme will run until 1999.

(14) To assess the performance of alternative refrigerants in building air conditioning systems and to provide information and guidance on their use, including the implications for energy efficiency and greenhouse gas emissions. Final results are to be published in early 1998.

3 Specific Environmental Hazards

3.1 Water

Objectives

● To protect water sources and supplies from biological and chemical contamination.

● To secure, on a sustainable basis, the continued availability of water for human consumption of a quality at least consistent with the World Health Organization (WHO) guidelines.

● To reduce the incidence of waterborne microbial diseases.

● To reduce exposure through drinking-water to toxic chemicals from industry and agriculture.

(EHAPE para 158)

Basis for action

Standards and tests

1. Over 99% of the population in the UK receives mains water supplies. These supplies are provided by private companies in England and Wales, by public water authorities in Scotland, and by Central Government in Northern Ireland; all are required to meet the same quality standards. The quality of these supplies is very high and all are safe to drink.

2. These supplies are tested regularly:

in England and Wales, the DWI checks that water companies supply wholesome drinking water which complies with the requirements of the Regulations. An annual report is published by the Chief Inspector. He reported that in 1995[33] 99.5% of the nearly 3.2 million of these tests complied with the relevant drinking water quality standards, which include microbiological, chemical, physical and aesthetic parameters. Where companies fail to meet standards the DWI will investigate and may initiate enforcement action;

in Northern Ireland in 1994, 98% of 125,000 tests complied with relevant drinking water standards; and

in Scotland, the SO carries out the checking and publishes an annual report; the comparable figures for 1994 were 98.7% of over 240,000 tests.

3. Some of the standards are stricter than those in the EC *Drinking Water Directive (80/778/EEC)*[175], and have been set on health grounds to provide additional protection to public health. The remaining standards

are in line with the requirements of the Directive. Samples to determine compliance with the standards are taken from consumers' taps as this provides the best protection to human health.

4. The most important standard for drinking water supplies is that for **coliform organisms**. Coliforms are not themselves usually harmful when ingested but they are important indicator organisms and if found in drinking water could indicate that other harmful bacteria could possibly be present. Consequently every detection of coliforms is immediately investigated by water undertakers and, when necessary, remedial action is taken. Some detections of coliforms are a consequence of the unhygienic condition of some consumers' pipework and taps.

5. The percentage of test results in water supply zones complying with the coliform standard has improved:

– in England and Wales, from 98.0% in 1990 to 99.3% in 1995 as a result of water undertakers completing improvement programmes; and

– in Scotland, from 93.1% in 1991 to 97.7% in 1994.

Comparable data will not be available for Northern Ireland until the end of 1996.

6. UK Regulations require that water supplies must not contain any element, organism or substance at a concentration which would be detrimental to public health. There are standards for 55 parameters. In the case of cryptosporidium, for which no standard is specified in the Regulations, comprehensive advice is

given in the Second Report of the Group of Experts on Cryptosporidium in Water Supplies[28].

7. In a few cases where not all standards have been met all of the time, the relevant Secretary of State has usually accepted undertakings from water suppliers to carry out the necessary improvements. Between 1989 and 1995 water suppliers in England and Wales spent an estimated £2.6 billion on these improvements. Most were complete by the end of 1995. The comparable expenditure in Northern Ireland between 1989 and 1995 was £55 million. The figure for Scotland was £388 million between 1990 and 1995.

8. However, in parts of the UK it is necessary to rehabilitate substantial lengths of water distribution mains: for such areas the timescales for achieving significant improvements in quality, primarily aesthetic improvements, are longer than for those which only require improvements at a treatment plant.

Lead pipes

9. Some older properties are connected to the water mains by lead service pipes or have internal lead plumbing. Certain types of water can dissolve lead from such lead pipes. The DWI has issued a leaflet which gives consumers advice in plain English on lead in drinking water, especially about how to find out whether they have lead pipes; how to find out if they have high lead concentrations; and what to do to reduce lead concentrations in the short term. In England and Wales, a Government funded study reported in 1992 on the extent of lead pipework, the effectiveness of alternative solutions for tackling lead, and the cost of lead pipe replacement programmes needed to meet the existing standard and possible future revisions to the standard. This study has helped inform Government policy on lead in drinking water. In the areas affected, water suppliers are installing treatment to reduce the amount of lead dissolved from lead water pipes. All planned work in England and Wales was completed by the beginning of 1996; the need for further work is being considered in certain areas. In most instances, treatment will reduce lead levels in drinking water *at the tap* to levels not exceeding 25-30 µg/l.

10. A lead survey assessment for Northern Ireland was completed early in 1996 and the results are currently being considered. This study will assist in the further improvement of measures to reduce lead levels in Northern Ireland water supplies. Replacement of householders' lead pipes may attract grant aid from the Northern Ireland Housing Executive.

11. In 1992, SO made a commitment to conduct a review by mid 1993 of public exposure to lead in drinking water. The review was delayed to take account of the revised guidelines on lead levels in drinking water, published by the WHO in 1993, and the proposed revision to the Drinking Water Directive[170], published in May 1995. The review made four recommendations:

(i)   The current lead standard and the associated regulatory duties to take measures to reduce lead in drinking water be continued meantime;

(ii) Local authorities should continue to identify households in their area with lead plumbing and continue to make repair grants available;

(iii) An approach be made to the Health Education Board for Scotland to encourage them to include reference to the dangers of lead in drinking water, and the means of reducing them, in future publications; and

(iv) An objective for the forthcoming negotiations on the proposals for a revised Drinking Water Directive should be that the long-term standard for lead is consistent with the scientific basis of WHO guidelines (as for other health based priorities also set on the basis of the WHO guideline values).

12. Replacement of householders' lead pipes may attract a grant from local authorities or central Government.

13. Some water suppliers also have programmes to replace their parts of lead service pipes to further reduce the exposure of consumers to lead. All water suppliers are obliged to replace their part of a lead service pipe when requested to do so by a householder who has replaced his part of any lead plumbing.

Pesticides in water

14. Government policy is to limit the amount of pesticides used to the minimum necessary for the effective control of pests compatible with the protection of human health and the environment. This is achieved through the rigorous approval and review of products, through guidance to users and through research and development. The standard for individual pesticides in drinking water supplies of 0.1µg/l is that of the EC Directive. This standard is precautionary and is not based on the health effect of individual substances.

15. Although some pesticides have been detected in some drinking water supplies at levels which exceed

the standard, these exceedances have not been at levels harmful to public health. Where the standard is exceeded, water suppliers have programmes to install treatment to reduce pesticide concentrations. Most of these programmes were completed by the beginning of 1996; the estimated total cost was £1 billion. Already there has been a reduction of 35% between 1991 and 1995 in the number of water supply zones not complying with the pesticides standard in England and Wales. This can be attributed to a combination of the completion of improvement programmes by water suppliers and to lower pesticide usage. The action taken has included withdrawal of approvals of non-agricultural uses of atrazine and simazine, and initiatives to encourage best practice in the use of agricultural pesticides such as isoproturon.

Nitrate Pollution

16. Although nitrate reaches water bodies from a number of sources, research evidence[125] indicates that agriculture is the main source. Other sources such as sewage effluent typically make only a minor contribution to nitrate loads in surface waters at a time when the nitrate concentration exceeds 50mg/l, the standard which applies to drinking water. The Government has a broad package of measures to control nitrate pollution from agriculture, such as: Nitrate Sensitive Areas under the *EC Agri-Environment Regulation (EEC/2078/92)*; and publication of the codes of Good Agricultural Practice[19, 20, 23] to help farmers reduce nitrate pollution in water.

17. In addition, 68 Nitrate Vulnerable Zones have been designated in England and Wales (out of 70 proposed at the time of the public consultation draft[144] of this UK NEHAP) as part of our implementation of the *EC Nitrate Directive*[171] concerning the protection of waters against pollution caused by nitrates from agricultural sources. A consultation paper was issued in November 1995 on the action programme measures to be established in the Zones to reduce agricultural nitrate pollution, The Government expects to establish the action programme later this year (1996). The Government has also announced that one Nitrate Vulnerable Zone will be designated in Scotland when regulations to transpose the Directive are made, later in 1996.

18. MAFF also maintains a substantial programme of nitrate research and development which helps to provide the basis for a comprehensive range of advice to farmers on sensible nitrate practice through such publications as its *Fertiliser Recommendations*[51]. A substantial programme of research into eutrophication in the Ythan estuary is being undertaken by the

SO. Under the *Urban Waste Water Treatment (England and Wales) Regulations 1994*[145] water companies may be required to undertake nitrate removal from certain sewage discharges into any area identified under the Regulations as a Sensitive Area (nitrate). Corresponding Regulations are also in force in Scotland.

19. The standard for nitrate in drinking water is 50mg/l as NO_3. Some water sources contain nitrate concentrations above 50mg/l and the water suppliers have installed additional treatment to achieve compliance with the standard: no such sources are in Northern Ireland or Scotland. Already, as a consequence of the completion of investment programmes between 1991 and 1995, a 70% reduction has been reported in the number of supply zones in England and Wales not complying with the standard. No confirmed cases of infantile methaemoglobinaemia attributable to nitrates in water have been reported in the UK since 1972.

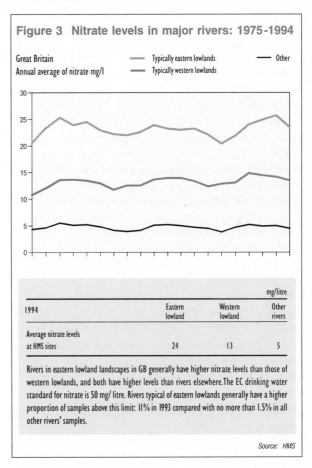

Figure 3   Nitrate levels in major rivers: 1975-1994

Great Britain
Annual average of nitrate mg/l

— Typically eastern lowlands
— Typically western lowlands
— Other

1994	Eastern lowland	Western lowland	Other rivers
			mg/litre
Average nitrate levels at HMS sites	24	13	5

Rivers in eastern lowland landscapes in GB generally have higher nitrate levels than those of western lowlands, and both have higher levels than rivers elsewhere. The EC drinking water standard for nitrate is 50 mg/ litre. Rivers typical of eastern lowlands generally have a higher proportion of samples above this limit: 11% in 1993 compared with no more than 1.5% in all other rivers' samples.

Source: HMS

Private water supplies

20. The remainder of drinking water supplies in the UK are private supplies. These can be drawn from lakes, streams, rivers, springs, wells or boreholes. They are usually found in remote and sparsely

populated areas, in which there can be microbiological contamination and local problems with nitrate levels. Regulations govern the quality of these supplies, also based on the requirements of the EC Drinking Water Directive. In England and Wales, the quality of these supplies is monitored by local authorities, who have powers to require improvements to be made where there is a risk to public health. In Northern Ireland, the regulation of private supplies is the responsibility of the DoENI.

21. The one time NRA, now part of the EA, produced a policy for groundwater to protect groundwater sources, including private water supplies. A similar policy for the protection of groundwater (the groundwater Protection Policy for Scotland) was produced by the Association of Directors and River Inspectors of Scotland.

Revision to EC Drinking Water Directive

22. In May 1995, the EC published proposals[70] for revisions to the current Drinking Water Directive, which the UK will be considering with other Members of the EU. The UK view is that standards in the Directive should be based, where possible, on the best scientific and medical knowledge available and on a full analysis of the costs and benefits but otherwise on the precautionary principle. The Commission's proposals include measures that would require Member States to reduce still further exposure to lead in drinking water.

Sewerage and sewage treatment

23. The UK has the highest percentage connection rate to sewers of any country in the EU (96%). The UK also has one of the highest levels of provision of sewage treatment with that from 83% of the population treated, mostly to secondary treatment standards. However, coastal discharges in the UK have traditionally been untreated except for simple screening.

24. In 1990, the Government announced its intention that, in future, all significant discharges of sewage would be treated. This policy is being taken forward through implementation of the EC's Urban Waste Water Treatment Directive[177].

25. Implementation of the Urban Waste Water Treatment Directive will ensure that all significant discharges of sewage are treated over a timetable spread from 1998 to 2005. In order to meet the requirements of the Directive, the UK water industry expects to invest £8 billion on sewage collection,

treatment and disposal between 1995 and 2005. Of the £8 billion, about £1.6 billion will be spent in Scotland and about £290 million in Northern Ireland. This expenditure is over and above the £17 billion being spent by the water industry on other improvements to water and sewerage services over the next decade. The *Urban Waste Water Treatment (England and Wales) Regulations 1994*[145] and the corresponding Regulations came into force in Scotland on 30 November 1994, and in Northern Ireland on 1 March 1995. The Environment Agencies will be required to monitor discharges from urban waste water treatment plants to verify compliance with the Regulations.

Water resources management

26. Water resources in the UK have been adequate to meet demands for most water supply purposes for many years. However, the exceptionally low rainfall over much of the country in the summer of 1995, which has persisted in some parts - notably the Pennines - into 1996, has caused some concern. In England and Wales, the developing situation has been closely monitored by the then NRA (now the EA) in conjunction with the water companies. Various short and longer term schemes have been put in place to reinforce supplies and there were no interruptions to public supplies in 1995 and no expectation of any in 1996. The Government is watching the position closely to ensure that all necessary action is taken to maintain supplies if drought continues.

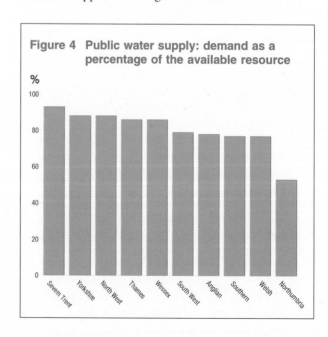

Figure 4 Public water supply: demand as a percentage of the available resource

27. Leakage from water distribution systems has received considerable attention as a result of the drought. The water service companies in England and

Wales have committed themselves to seeking to achieve the lowest levels of leakage that best practice suggests are both technically feasible and economically sensible. The Government can impose statutory targets for leakage on water companies if the Director General of Water Services requests it.

28. The Secretary of State for the Environment announced in September 1995 a longer term review of the lessons to be learnt from that summer's drought. This is being carried out in consultation with the EA, the Office of Water Services and representatives of the water companies. The review is looking at changes in the pattern of demand for water and the approach to demand management, and at progress with making water supply systems more flexible. It is also considering the implications of climate change. The outcome of the review will be published in 1996.

29. During 1994, SO carried out an assessment of demands and resources for public water supplies in Scotland covering the period 1991 to 2016. A report on this assessment was published in July 1995[12]. The report shows that, at national and regional levels, resources are more than sufficient to meet average demands for public water supplies beyond the year 2016. However, around the end of 1995, Scotland experienced extreme cold temperatures leading to extensive pipe bursts and abnormally high demands for water. The Government has set up a working group to investigate the lessons to be learnt from this event.

30. In 1994, a comprehensive water demand and resource study for Northern Ireland was completed resulting in the Water Resource Strategy. The Strategy extends to the year 2021 and involves a combination of new service developments, rationalisation of existing systems, closure of uneconomic sources and reduction of leakage levels. Staged capital expenditure in excess of £400 million is required in the period up to 2021.

31. In recent years, new water resources schemes in the UK have been designed to include recreational activity and promote nature conservation. This includes new wetland and water habitats for flora and fauna, facilities and venues for recreation and amenity, forming Areas of Outstanding Natural Beauty (AONBs), and the creation of Sites of Special Scientific Interest (SSSIs). Some reservoirs attract over 100,000 visitors a year for recreational purposes.

32. Before the creation of the NRA, some abstraction schemes did not take due account of the effect on rivers. To remedy this the NRA (now the EA) identified 40 low flow rivers in England and Wales where abstractions have severely depleted low flows and where remedial action is necessary. Ten flow

restoration schemes have been completed, others are under way and the remainder are at an advanced planning stage.

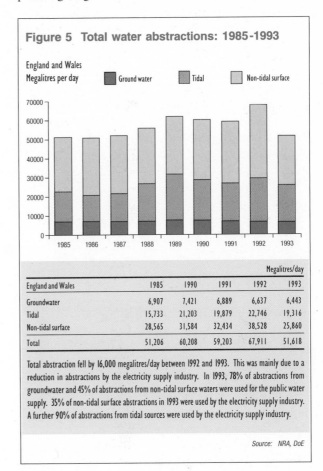

Figure 5 Total water abstractions: 1985-1993

England and Wales
Megalitres per day — Ground water, Tidal, Non-tidal surface

England and Wales	1985	1990	1991	1992	1993
Groundwater	6,907	7,421	6,889	6,637	6,443
Tidal	15,733	21,203	19,879	22,746	19,316
Non-tidal surface	28,565	31,584	32,434	38,528	25,860
Total	51,206	60,208	59,203	67,911	51,618

Megalitres/day

Total abstraction fell by 16,000 megalitres/day between 1992 and 1993. This was mainly due to a reduction in abstractions by the electricity supply industry. In 1993, 78% of abstractions from groundwater and 45% of abstractions from non-tidal surface waters were used for the public water supply. 35% of non-tidal surface abstractions in 1993 were used by the electricity supply industry. A further 90% of abstractions from tidal sources were used by the electricity supply industry.

Source: NRA, DoE

33. In Scotland, where water is generally more plentiful, selective controls over abstraction for irrigation are available. The Government announced in November 1994 its intention to introduce wider, but still selective, powers to control abstractions in the light of the European Commission's proposals for a Groundwater Action Programme.

34. In view of the ample natural water resources in Northern Ireland, it has not, so far, been considered necessary to introduce general abstraction controls but the need for selective controls is being considered.

Pollution emergencies

35. The EA has comprehensive arrangements to deal with emergencies. Notification of incidents has increased following the introduction of a free 24-hour emergency telephone line to eight regional control rooms (about 30,000 calls were received in 1994). Plans which are tested on a regular basis, have been developed to protect drinking water supplies and respond to other public health threats.

36. The number of major pollution incidents fell by 65% between 1990 (NRA's first full year of operation) and 1994, reflecting the effectiveness of NRA's activities in encouraging better preventative measures, enforcement and emergency planning. The EA will continue the NRA's aim to attend pollution emergencies within two hours during normal working hours and four hours at other times. In 1994/95, 93% of major and 91% of significant incidents were attended in target time, most well within the specified periods. The comparable figures for 1993/94 were 92% and 86% respectively.

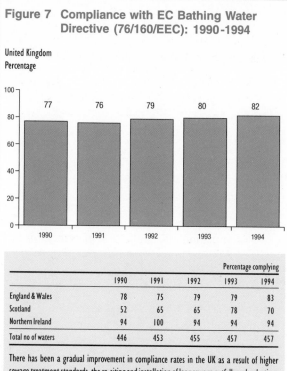

Figure 7   Compliance with EC Bathing Water Directive (76/160/EEC): 1990-1994

United Kingdom Percentage

| | 1990 | 1991 | 1992 | 1993 | 1994 |
					Percentage complying
England & Wales	78	75	79	79	83
Scotland	52	65	65	78	70
Northern Ireland	94	100	94	94	94
Total no of waters	446	453	455	457	457

There has been a gradual improvement in compliance rates in the UK as a result of higher sewage treatment standards, the re-siting and installation of long sewage outfalls and reductions in storm overflow. To comply with the Directive, at least 95% of samples taken must not exceed the mandatory limit values set down in the Directive for total and faecal coliforms. These parameters are considered to be the most important indicators of sewage contamination.

Source: NRA, SOEnD, DoE(NI)

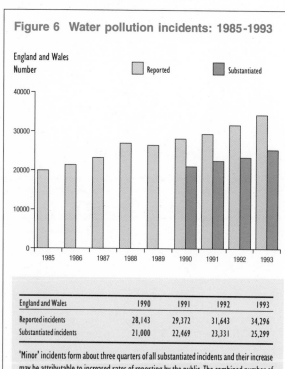

Figure 6   Water pollution incidents: 1985-1993

England and Wales Number

Reported   Substantiated

England and Wales	1990	1991	1992	1993
Reported incidents	28,143	29,372	31,643	34,296
Substantiated incidents	21,000	22,469	23,331	25,299

'Minor' incidents form about three quarters of all substantiated incidents and their increase may be attributable to increased rates of reporting by the public. The combined number of 'major' and 'significant' incidents has remained broadly level over the last three years and may provide a more meaningful indication of actual trends in pollution incidents, being less affected by any changes in public reporting rates.

Source: NRA

Bathing Water

37. A recent UK report[63] has shown that the EC mandatory bacteria standards for bathing waters are adequate to protect health. Almost 90% of identified bathing waters in the UK already meet or exceed these standards. A £2 billion programme of improvements is well under way to bring the remaining bathing waters into compliance soon.

Charging for water

38. The availability of a supply of good quality water for drinking and hygienic purposes is important for health and well-being. However, the provision of water and sanitation in an urban society requires a complex and costly infrastructure which has to be paid for. Whilst the Government recognises that there is some discussion about the best basis of charging for water, and concern about disconnections, it considers that these are matters for water companies in England and Wales to manage with guidance from the regulator, who has tightened the limits on charge increases. In Scotland, the new public water authorities are required to agree charges schemes with the Scottish Water and Sewerage Customers Council, a body established in 1995 to protect consumers' interests.

39. In England and Wales, water companies are considering the most appropriate basis for charging for water in their respective areas. The Office of Water Services (OFWAT) issued Guidelines on Debt and Disconnection in 1992, since when the number of disconnections has steadily fallen. For those on Income Support there is also a scheme for the direct payment of water charges to prevent disconnection when other options have failed.

Actions: Group 2

40. The following Group 2 actions are planned:

(1) In England and Wales installation of further treatment to reduce lead levels in drinking water to meet the requirements of UK Regulations has been largely completed; the remaining work will be completed by September 1997. Gradual replacement of lead communication pipes by water suppliers will continue.

(2) By 2005, completion of £8 billion investment programme to meet Urban Waste Water Treatment Directive.

(3) Microbiological test data will be made available for Northern Ireland by the end of 1996.

(4) From 1996 to 2001, the Water Service of DoENI plans to invest £102 million in new works, with a further £90 million scheduled for later years.

(5) The Government's decisions on actions to reduce lead levels in Northern Ireland, including its re-examination of the rate of replacement of lead communication pipes, will be published in 1997.

Actions: Group 3

41. The following Group 3 actions are proposed:

(1) All relevant sewage discharges to designated sensitive areas (nitrate) to comply with the required level of treatment in the *Urban Waste Water Treatment Directive* by the required deadline.

(2) The outcome of the review of the lessons to be learnt from the 1995 drought will be published later in 1996.

(3) As the first priority of the Northern Ireland Water Resource Strategy, a new source of supply for the eastern part of Northern Ireland will be completed by 2003 at a cost of £50 million.

(4) The EA will spend over £4 million on flow restoration schemes in 1996/97, with further expenditure thereafter.

(5) Complete remainder of the bathing water improvement programme as soon as possible.

3.2 Air Quality

Objectives

- To provide information on indoor and outdoor air pollution levels throughout Europe, especially in urban areas.

- To adopt the measures required to bring, by a date to be specified nationally, air pollution levels below the health-related WHO air quality guidelines.

(EHAPE para 168)

Basis for action

1. This section deals separately with indoor and outdoor air quality because the basis for action and the actions themselves differ greatly. Indoors the air quality can be controlled by those in charge of the building. Outdoors the air quality depends on the combined effects of all sources of airborne pollution.

Indoor air quality

Impact on health

2. In the UK, on average, people spend 90% of their time indoors, and three quarters of that in the home[I]. Therefore, exposure to indoor air pollutants may have a impact on the health and well-being of the building occupants. Rates of respiratory disease and incidence of allergic responses such as asthma have increased in recent years, and there is concern that some of this increase can be associated with changes in the indoor environment.

3. Indoor pollutants arise from the outdoor air, seepage through the ground, the materials of construction, fittings and fixtures, activities within the building and the occupants themselves. The indoor air pollutants posing the greatest hazard include carbon monoxide (responsible for about 100 accidental deaths per year), radon (see Section 3.5) and environmental tobacco smoke (both of which are implicated in the incidence of cancer). Also of concern are nitrogen dioxide (from use of gas cookers), house-dust mites, and VOCs (all of which are implicated in the incidence of respiratory disease, especially in children), fungi, bacteria, and asbestos.

Knowledge and research

4. The risks from all these pollutants have recently been reviewed[68] and form the basis for action to improve indoor air quality. However, there is uncertainty about the actual levels of these pollutants in UK homes, and the effect of those levels on health. The acquisition of information on the levels and effects of indoor air pollutants is essential in order to set targets for the reduction of levels of these pollutants. The Government is currently funding a substantial programme of research and development which is intended to:

- develop the necessary methodology to sample and examine indoor air;

- apply that methodology to the monitoring of representative samples of UK homes in order to establish the levels of pollutants that exist;

- assess the likely consequences for health and well-being of exposure to both peak and typical levels of pollutants found in homes, paying particular attention to their significance for susceptible groups such as babies or the elderly;

- measure the rate of pollutant emission from particular sources, such as construction materials and do-it-yourself products; and

- develop and investigate strategies for reducing the concentrations of particular indoor air pollutants where necessary, and improving indoor air quality overall.

[I] A typical adult in work will spend 60% of his time at home, 25% at the workplace, 5% in public places, shops, leisure pursuits etc, 5% in transport and 5% outdoors. Old people, young children and their mothers typically spend more time in the home.

Smoking in public places

5. The Government has accepted the advice of the Independent Scientific Committee on Smoking and Health[57] that "non-smoking should be regarded as the norm in enclosed areas frequented by the public or employees, special provision being made for smokers rather than vice versa". The Government is committed to creating a non-smoking environment, with facilities where appropriate for those who wish to smoke, by encouraging the implementation of suitable policies on smoking in public places. It has published a Code of Practice[124] and guidance on suitable smoking policies for public places to help achieve this objective. A recent survey for the DoE[122, 123] has shown that an increasing number of public places are implementing policies on smoking. The Government is currently looking at further ways of encouraging this trend.

Outdoor air quality

Impact on health

6. Concentrations of air pollutants in the UK vary from region to region and from day to day. On occasion concentrations are significantly raised and during such air pollution episodes some adverse effects on health occur. These include an increase of admissions to hospital for treatment of cardiovascular and respiratory disorders. It is also likely that deaths from cardio-respiratory disorders increase on days when concentrations of particles are raised. It is likely that these deaths occur among those who already suffer from cardio-respiratory disease and that healthy individuals are not affected. Deaths among the elderly may be brought forward during pollution episodes, but it is not clear by how long.

7. Studies of the effects of air pollution episodes (such as occurred in London in 1991) have not revealed such marked effects on the health of asthmatic patients as on those with other respiratory disorders; however, those suffering from severe asthma have been shown to be adversely affected during air pollution episodes. A report[13] by the Committee on the Medical Effects of Air Pollutants has confirmed that most of the available evidence does not indicate that non-biological air pollution causes asthma in previously healthy individuals, although it may aggravate attacks in people who already have asthma.

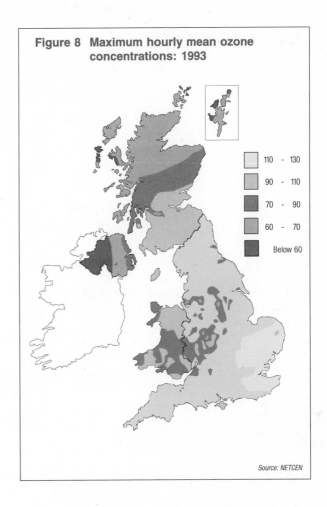

Figure 8 Maximum hourly mean ozone concentrations: 1993

110 – 130
90 – 110
70 – 90
60 – 70
Below 60

Source: NETCEN

8. Air quality in the UK has been improving in recent years and these improvements are set to continue over the next decade. The innovative new systems for dealing with industrial pollution introduced by the Environmental Protection Act 1990 (see Section 2.3), new vehicle standards, and other measures aimed at mitigating the environmental impacts of traffic will lead to substantial reductions in emissions of many of the more important pollutants in the next decade. However, additional measures will be necessary to ensure that these benefits are not eroded by further growth in road traffic. The UK expects to meet its existing international commitments[II] for reductions in emissions of NOx, SO_2 and VOCs. There remain, however, significant challenges and uncertainties. WHO Guidelines for some pollutants are still exceeded in the UK during summer and winter pollution episodes.

II   Under the EC Large Combustion Plant Directive and the UNECE Protocols on NOx, VOCs and Sulphur with the Convention on Long Range Transboundary Air Pollution.

A National Air Quality Strategy

9. Under the Environment Act 1995, the Secretary of State will shortly publish a National Air Quality Strategy, in line with the proposals made in *Air Quality: Meeting The Challenge*[7]. This strategy will include:

- a framework of ambient air quality standards, objectives and targets for the major air pollutants: benzene; ozone; 1,3-butadiene; carbon monoxide; sulphur dioxide; particles; nitrogen dioxide; and lead (national standards and targets are being set, taking account of advice from the Expert Panel on Air Quality Standards and WHO); and

- a description of how the Government envisages these objectives and targets will be met, and over what timescale.

Local air quality management

10. Clear standards and targets are essential, but they must also be supported by effective means of achieving them. At present, the EA, the SEPA and local authorities have obligations to observe appropriate standards in authorising industrial emissions. The Environment Act 1995 created a new system of local air quality management. Local authorities have a duty to carry out periodic reviews of air quality within their boundaries and make action plans in areas where standards and objectives are not met, and the Environment Agencies will also play a role. Local authorities will have to consult widely in preparing their plans – with neighbouring authorities, the EA, the SEPA, highway authorities, industry, other appropriate bodies and the public.

11. The Environment Act includes wide regulation-making powers to provide for any new tools which local authorities might need to manage air quality. This could, for example, provide for regulations to enable local authorities to undertake vehicle emission checks. Such regulations could provide for spot fines for offenders. DOT is conducting trials of such proposals with the help of selected local authorities.

12. Local authority actions will be carefully targeted, and based on the recognition that action at the local rather than the national level may often be the most cost-effective way to tackle potential local air quality problems.

Vehicle emissions

13. In the *Sustainable Development Strategy*[133] the Government made it clear that improvements in air quality depended to a large extent on improvements in the transport sector. Vehicle emissions are expected to fall dramatically over the next decade, as the current vehicle fleet is replaced by vehicles conforming to the tighter standards which have been brought in since 1992. The National Air Quality Strategy will include a chapter outlining the further measures which will be taken to reduce emissions from this sector. It is expected that improvements in vehicle and fuel technology will have the largest part to play. However, an effective strategic policy must also incorporate:

- tighter controls on the existing vehicle fleet, its management and operation;

- development of environmental responsibilities by fleet operators, particularly public service fleet operators, and by the public at large, in transport and vehicle use; and

- changes in planning and transport policies which, over the long term, would reduce the need to travel.

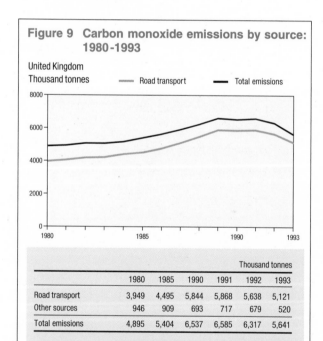

Figure 9   Carbon monoxide emissions by source: 1980-1993

United Kingdom
Thousand tonnes

— Road transport   — Total emissions

		Thousand tonnes
	1980	1985	1990	1991	1992	1993
Road transport	3,949	4,495	5,844	5,868	5,638	5,121
Other sources	946	909	693	717	679	520
Total emissions	4,895	5,404	6,537	6,585	6,317	5,641

Total carbon monoxide (CO) emissions fell by nearly 900,000 tonnes between 1990 and 1993. Emissions from road transport now constitute over 90% of all emissions of CO. Emissions from this source rose substantially in the 1970s and 1980s but since 1991 they have begun to fall because of the increase in diesel cars which emit less CO than petrol-fuelled cars. Emissions are likely to fall further as a result of the introduction of catalytic converters, which became mandatory for new petrol-fuelled cars in 1993.

Source: NETCEN

Actions: Groups 2 and 3

Indoor air quality

14. The following Groups 2 and 3 actions are planned:

    (1) Stimulate effective action to reduce levels of key air pollutants in homes.

    (2) Undertake a programme of indoor air quality research and development at a cost of about £1.3m a year up to 1999.

    (3) Produce and disseminate advice to building professionals and the public on how to improve indoor air quality in the non-workplace environment.

    (4) Consider options for control of indoor air quality, using a cost benefit analysis, including alterations to building regulations, the Housing Fitness Standard, gas safety legislation or product controls.

    (5) Continue the current publicity campaign on the dangers of carbon monoxide from unflued combustion appliances, and investigate the efficacy of carbon monoxide detectors.

    (6) Achieve a 10% increase on 1995 figures in the number of establishments with effective non-smoking policies in place by 1998, monitor progress with a survey in 1998, and advise the public on the risks to children's health from environmental tobacco smoke.

    (7) Publicise advice on practical measures to reduce levels of house dust mite allergen in homes and conduct research into strategies for reducing levels of mites in homes.

Outdoor air quality

15. The following Groups 2 and 3 actions are planned:

    (1) Publish a National Air Quality Strategy in 1996, including standards, targets and objectives for individual pollutants and a timetable for achieving these objectives. The Strategy will include chapters on industry, transport, monitoring, Europe and local government, setting out the measures to be taken to meet the standards.

    (2) Achieve the Government's objective that air quality targets should be met in the UK by the year 2005.

    (3) Fulfil international commitments for reductions in emissions of NO_2, SO_2 and volatile organic compounds.

    (4) Expand the national air quality monitoring network to at least 80 sites by the end of 1996.

    (5) Create a national archive of UK air quality data on the Internet to improve public access to air quality information by the end of 1996.

3.3 Food

Objectives

- To reduce the incidence of and, if possible, eliminate diseases associated with contaminated food.

- To ensure that food safety is put first in each process and in each part of the food production and distribution chain, from primary producer to consumer.

- To improve public awareness of food safety and hygiene.

(EHAPE para 185)

Basis for action

Food Policy

1. Food can present risks to health both through microbial contamination and also through the presence of toxic chemicals or radioactive elements. Central Government carries out extensive surveillance and research to give a sound scientific basis for assessing the risks and for managing them in a proportionate way through regulation, education or advice. Nutrition is considered to be outside the scope of the UK NEHAP.

2. The key piece of UK legislation is the Food Safety Act 1990, which controls the composition and safety of food in its preparation and sale. Within the framework provided by the Act, more detailed requirements are contained in Regulations which, among other things, implement EC legislation. In Northern Ireland, the Food Safety (Northern Ireland) Order 1991 and regulations made under it contain similar provisions. The *enforcement* of the major part of food law is the responsibility of local authorities: Central Government issues statutory codes of practice to guide them.

3. Within local authorities, food law enforcement is carried out by either Trading Standards Officers or Environmental Health Departments, or by public protection departments in Wales. The Food Safety Act gives inspectors wide powers to inspect any stage of the production, manufacturing and distribution chain, and take samples for testing. Inspectors have powers to issue warnings, improvement notices or take prosecutions against businesses. For breaches of the food law, the courts can inflict heavy penalties, including the closure of a food business. There is great reliance on regular routine inspection of establishments to achieve the laid down standards; giving advice forms a large part of the work. On food safety issues, the Local Authority Coordinating Body on Food and Trading Standards (LACOTS) acts as the body for local authorities to ensure consistency of enforcement.

4. The Meat Hygiene Service, an executive agency of MAFF has responsibility for hygiene (and welfare) inspection and enforcement in licensed fresh meat, poultry meat, and game establishments in Great Britain.

Chemicals and radioactivity

5. Chemicals, such as food additives, deliberately added to food are only approved for use after an extensive evaluation of both the need and safety by independent expert committees. The area is highly regulated with several EC Directives which have been implemented into UK regulations. Limits for some chemical contaminants are contained in long established UK regulations. In the case of pesticide and veterinary residues, limits are being established in a series of EC Directives. There is tight regulation of emissions of radioactivity from nuclear establishments (see section 3.5 on Radiation). The risks to human health from emissions from nuclear installations are small (less than 1% of total population radiation exposure), compared with those from natural radioactivity.

Food surveillance

6. A comprehensive surveillance programme generates information on the level of contaminants and other residues in food. This information is then used to assess the dietary intakes of residues by the population in general or specific groups considered to be at a particular risk. The surveillance programme also ensures that statutory controls are being observed. Overall, about 140,000 analyses are carried out each year for a wide range of contaminants. The large

majority of results do not generate any concerns about risks to health. The results of this extensive surveillance programme are published in a range of MAFF reports including the monthly Food Safety Information Bulletin published jointly with DH. In Northern Ireland, surveys are sometimes expanded to obtain a more statistically meaningful sample.

Food-borne illness

7. A key part of the Government's action to reduce food borne illness is its major £2.8 million study of infectious intestinal disease (IID) in England. The purpose of the study is to establish the incidence, sources, causes and socio-economic costs of IID. The results of the study, which will be available in 1997, should provide a sound scientific basis for developing further strategies to reduce the risk of food borne illness. Surveys are also underway to provide much better data on levels of contamination in the food chain. Completion of the IID study is the priority target for action. Notified cases of food poisoning are reported in Chief Medical Officers' (CMO) annual reports[67, 87, 126, 148].

8. In Scotland, the Scottish Centre for Infection and Environmental Health (SCIEH) will undertake a similar exercise to study IID. It is proposed to build on the Centre's existing primary care surveillance of information consisting of selected general practitioner practices and extend this into a comprehensive surveillance scheme which will involve contracts with both general practitioners and laboratories. This will be a unique approach which will enhance surveillance in Scotland.

9. The SCIEH Weekly Report includes reports of statutory notifiable cases of food poisoning and also reports of samples of organisms responsible for food poisoning from laboratory sources. The annual reports of the CMO for Scotland include a section on the epidemiology of gastro-intestinal infections in Scotland.

10. In Wales, the Welsh Food Microbiological Forum has been set up to coordinate the food sampling programmes of local authorities and Public Health Laboratories. The Forum has the objectives of establishing the picture of the microbiological quality of foods across Wales, alerting local authorities to areas of variability in microbiological quality which merit local attention, documenting factors affecting microbiological quality, and recording long term trends in microbiological quality. So far, data have been collected on a random sample of premises which supply a wide range of different types of food.

11. The ACMSF reports on Vacuum Packaging and Associated Processes (1992)[4], Salmonella in Eggs (1993)[3], Campylobacter (1993)[1], Verocytotoxin-producing Escherichia coli (1995)[5], and Poultry Meat (1996)[2] contain recommendations to Government, industry, public health bodies and consumers for research to fill gaps in knowledge, and measures to prevent and control food borne microbiological illness. The Government has accepted the recommendations addressed to it in these reports and has taken action to implement them. The ACMSF is currently reviewing food borne viral infections and microbial antibiotic resistance in relation to food safety.

Food Safety

12. Everyone involved in the food chain must carry their responsibility for helping to ensure that food is safe. The Government has therefore promoted the Hazard Analysis Critical Control Point approach as the best way of preventing food-borne illness. The EC Directive 93/43/EEC on the hygiene of foodstuffs and a number of other product specific hygiene Directives introduce a provision requiring business operators to identify activities which have the potential to cause harm to consumers and ensure that sufficient controls are in place to minimise such risks. These Directives simplified legislation and replaced several earlier sets of regulations. The new provision links food hygiene to the level of risk and requires that, where risk is high, greater precautions should be taken to avoid any risk of contamination of foodstuffs. As part of this approach, business operators must assess hazards within their production areas that may lead to food problems, pinpoint those areas that are critical to ensuring food safety, and maintain and review all controls. There should be benefits to food businesses from this hazard analysis system. The Compliance Cost Assessment shows that costs to business will be influenced by the number of processes and the unit cost of the analysis. The approach ensures that businesses take the action most appropriate to their own circumstances, while operating within the general framework and, in the case of product specific Directives, prescription laid down in accordance with EU law. It also gives a clear direction to government action and enables regulation to be combined with flexibility.

13. Anyone covered by the Food Safety (General Food Hygiene) Regulations 1995 must carry out operations safely and hygienically. The Regulations are enforced by local EHOs who must consider the risk to public health posed by particular activities when deciding what action to take. The Government

works closely with food organisations, the CIEH, and LACOTS to encourage a consistent approach. The LACOTS' coordinating role in achieving consistency and reasonable enforcement is seen as an important process in the early years of operating the new Regulations.

Food hygiene awareness

14. As part of the implementation of the new General Food Hygiene Regulations[55] several measures have been introduced to help food businesses. A number of publications have been produced, including general guidance notes and explanatory booklets[55-56], explaining the regulations and advising on the interpretation of risk-related provisions. The changes have been advertised and explained to businesses and enforcement officers through nationwide seminars and 'Roadshow' presentations. The Code of Practice[22] on inspections has been updated and voluntary Guides to Good Practice[74] have been prepared in collaboration with industry.

15. The Government also runs the *Foodsense Campaign* and gives financial support to the annual National Food Safety Week aimed at the general public. The campaign includes

> – the Foodsense leaflet *Food Safety* which contains tips and advice on shopping for food and storing and preparing it safely – well over 2.5 million copies have been distributed;

> – *Keeping Food Cool and Safe* which concentrates on safe refrigeration; and
>
> – the popular *Hy-Genie* range of educational materials which aims to promote food hygiene among primary school children.

Foodsense leaflets, which are free of charge, are widely available in the main supermarket chains. Additionally, local authorities also carry out publicity campaigns.

European cooperation

16. An EC Directive (93/5/EEC) establishes the procedures for the Commission to cooperate with Member States in the scientific examination of questions relating to food. Several tasks have now been completed under this arrangement including four on contaminants (aflatoxin, ochratoxin A, cadmium and nitrate). It is expected that the Commission will put forward further tasks on contaminants. In the furtherance of the European 'Health for All' Target 22, the UK has already made an input to two WHO-organised meetings on the reliable evaluation of low-level contamination of food. The UK is also actively involved with other European states in establishing a general standard for contaminants in food under the auspices of the Codex Committee on Food Additives and Contaminants and is also assisting the WHO in its risk assessment programme.

Actions: Group 2

17. The following Group 2 actions are planned:

(1) Complete and report on the IID study by Summer 1997 and consider the policy implications and the need for further targeted surveillance and research.

(2) Continue research to improve the characterisation of low level risk from chemical contaminants, thereby developing risk-based regulation and ensuring better use of resources.

(3) Continue to promote the risk management approach to food safety through, for example, contribution to a forthcoming EC review of food hygiene Directives.

(4) Continue the programme of work in hand to implement the recommendations of the ACMSF's reports.

(5) Continue the programme of national microbiological food surveillance coordinated by the MSFG to identify the need for action to ensure the microbiological safety of food.

3.4 Solid Wastes and Soil Pollution

Objectives

- To ensure the safe and nuisance-free disposal of (urban and rural) community and industrial waste, in order adequately to protect the health of workers and the public during collection, transportation, treatment and final disposal.

- To minimize waste production and promote recycling, reuse and energy recovery.

- To identify contaminated sites, assess the risks they pose to health and the environment and reduce or eliminate those risks deemed unacceptable.

(EHAPE para 200)

Basis for action

Policy on waste

1. The Government's policy on waste is based on a hierarchy of waste management options: the reduction of waste, its reuse wherever possible, recycling, composting and energy recovery, and finally disposal. However, there will always be certain wastes for which disposal is the most sensible environmental and economic option. The Government's policy is to make the best use of unavoidable waste, minimising the risk of pollution or harm to human health.

2. Control of waste disposal operations was first legislated for in the Control of Pollution Act 1974. A new and even more stringent system of waste management licensing for disposal of waste on land was brought into force on 1 May 1994 under Part II of the Environmental Protection Act 1990. The Act, and its associated regulations[146], impose strict controls on the landfill of waste. Disposal of waste at sea is controlled under the Food and Environment Protection Act 1985.

Reduction of waste

3. Waste minimisation is the most sustainable waste management option and is at the top of the hierarchy of waste management options set out in the Government's White Paper *Making Waste Work*[79]. The Government is promoting this option to both industry and householders. It has already held a conference, and a series of road shows aimed at getting the message to business. Promotional leaflets have been produced and a poster campaign is planned. The Environmental Technology Best Practice Programme[I]

(see also paragraphs 5 and 6 of Section 5.1) is advising business on how to reduce their waste. The *Going for Green* initiative[II] has responsibility for promoting the waste minimisation message to householders.

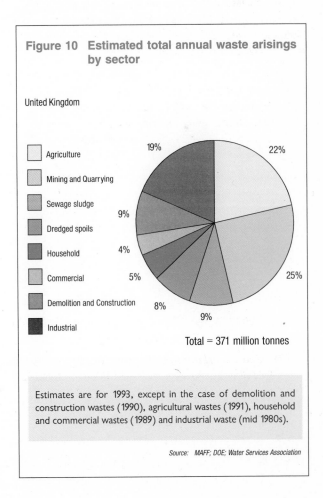

Figure 10 Estimated total annual waste arisings by sector

United Kingdom

- Agriculture
- Mining and Quarrying
- Sewage sludge
- Dredged spoils
- Household
- Commercial
- Demolition and Construction
- Industrial

19%   22%   9%   4%   25%   5%   8%   9%

Total = 371 million tonnes

Estimates are for 1993, except in the case of demolition and construction wastes (1990), agricultural wastes (1991), household and commercial wastes (1989) and industrial waste (mid 1980s).

Source: MAFF; DOE; Water Services Association

[I] Helpline number 0800 585794.

[II] *Going for Green*, PO Box 2100 Manchester M60 3GN.

Waste regulation

4. Since 1 April 1996 the EA and the SEPA have had responsibility for waste regulation. They use their statutory powers to licence waste management sites, set and enforce conditions on those sites, and prosecute waste pollution offences. A breach of the conditions of a waste management licence, for example by accepting wastes on a site which is not licensed to take them, can be a criminal offence. A conviction could result in the revocation of the licence. It is for the Environment Agencies to take action if they discover that such a breach has taken place.

5. Before a waste management licence can be granted, extensive consultation with relevant bodies must be carried out. The Environment Agencies must be satisfied that disposal operations will not harm human health or pollute the environment. Conditions are imposed in a licence to protect human health and the environment. These can include lists of wastes which can or cannot be accepted at a landfill, and the monitoring of groundwater and landfill gas (both while the site is operational and after its closure) until the appropriate Agency judges that the site is safe. Only once a site is judged to be safe will a licence holder be permitted to surrender his licence.

Waste collection

6. With some specific exceptions, waste collection authorities (WCAs) have a duty to collect household waste and, if requested, commercial waste. They may also collect industrial waste if requested. Household waste is collected, in the main, free of charge. WCAs can, however, charge for certain types of household waste, such as garden waste or large bulky items. A charge is made for the collection of commercial and industrial waste. However, many businesses have contracts with private sector companies instead.

Waste disposal

7. The 'duty of care', which was brought into effect in 1992 under the Environmental Protection Act 1990, requires all those who have control of waste to ensure that it is properly managed from production to disposal. Under the duty of care, each producer and handler of waste must ensure that waste is transferred only to those authorised to handle and dispose of it in a safe and legal way. The duty of care is designed to cut off the supply of waste to illegal operators, and to deter authorised operators from breaking the law. It establishes a system of documentary records to enable the Environment Agencies to trace waste movements from production to disposal.

Sewage sludge

8. In the UK, some 49% of sewage sludge is used on agricultural land. Controls under the Sludge (Use in Agriculture) Regulations 1989[121], and the associated Code of Practice[23] aim to ensure that: sludge use is compatible with good agricultural practice; the long term viability of agricultural activity is safeguarded; public nuisance and water pollution are avoided; and human, animal or plant health are not put at risk.

9. Wastes arising from agriculture are mainly recycled to land in the form of crop residues, slurries and manures. However, waste which may pose a health risk is disposed of in compliance with the EC Animal Waste Directive[153] and other domestic legislation.

Landfill

10. A high level of technological expertise in landfill has been built up in the UK. The geology in many areas is suitable for safely engineered landfilling, preventing the liquids (leachate) formed by landfill waste from seeping into water sources. A significant component of the EA's waste management research programme deals with the theory and practice of land filling. This has led to the publication of a series of research reports on different aspects of the biology and chemistry of landfill processes. DoE and the Agency are jointly in the process of publishing a series of Waste Management Papers on landfill design and operation.

11. The BRE investigates the performance of measures to protect buildings from the ingress of landfill gas, and evaluates on-site landfill gas measurement methods, so that risks posed to developments near landfills may be more fully understood. BRE also provides an advice service to customers on landfill gas hazards.

Incineration

12. Incineration is strictly controlled under the Environmental Protection Act 1990 and relevant subordinate legislation. Incineration processes are regulated either under the provisions for integrated pollution control by the EA for hazardous waste incinerators or incinerators taking more than one tonne of waste per hour, or under the air pollution control provisions by local authorities for smaller incinerators. Incineration at sea is prohibited.

13. The number of incinerators has gone down since 1991 and will continue to do so because of tightened emission limits set by EC Directives. Those which

remain will operate to a much higher environmental standard. For some wastes, such as highly flammable or toxic wastes, which are not suitable for landfilling, incineration is currently the only satisfactory way of dealing with them. Incineration is also useful as a way of treating wastes prior to landfilling. It destroys the materials in the waste which would produce methane.

14. No disposal method is without the potential to pollute, and incineration is no exception. Emissions from waste to energy plants contain toxic and acidic components and the bottom ash also contains pollutants, especially metals. But, overall, the pollution control standards for modern incinerators are extremely high, and incineration accounts for a diminishing share of airborne pollutants. Furthermore, a recent review of dioxin pollution carried out by the Committee on Toxicity concluded that there was unlikely to be a health risk from the current intake levels of dioxins. The Government will continue to monitor the health risks associated with dioxins, and the results will help regulatory authorities to set standards.

Hazardous wastes

15. Hazardous wastes require special attention. The Special Waste Regulations 1996 impose documentation and tracking requirements on the movement and disposal of wastes identified as having particular hazards. DoE has published guidance to determine those wastes which will be subject to the 1996 Regulations. The disposal of hazardous wastes is controlled through the waste management licensing system. Movement of hazardous wastes across international borders is the subject of international agreements. DoE is working with the United Nations, OECD and EU agencies to assist in the development of better methods for the characterisation of waste hazards.

Recycling

16. Recycling of waste reduces the need for landfill disposal. The Government encourages recycling where it is economically and environmentally beneficial. A number of measures were introduced in the Environmental Protection Act 1990 to promote the recycling of household waste. These include a requirement that all waste collection authorities produce waste recycling plans, and the introduction of the recycling credits scheme (an economic instrument providing financial support for recycling).

17. Since 1990, local authorities have introduced a range of schemes to help promote household waste recycling. The provision of banks for the collection of

a variety of materials such as glass, paper and cans is now commonplace, and many authorities have also introduced kerbside collection schemes.

Figure 11 Per capita recycling rates for selected materials: 1989-1993

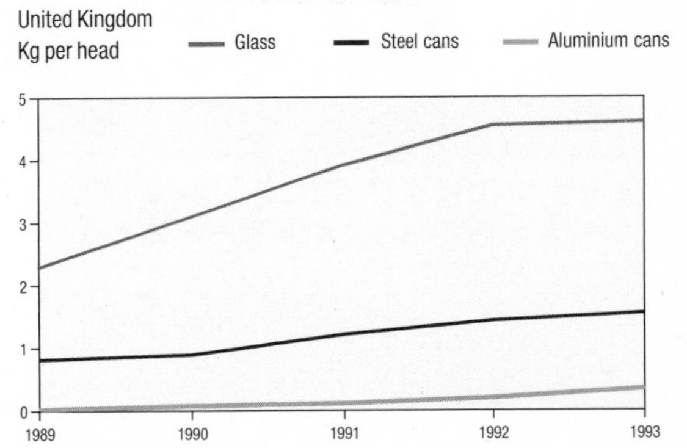

United Kingdom
Kg per head — Glass — Steel cans — Aluminium cans

		kg per head		
	1989	1990	1991	1992	1993
Steel cans	0.82	0.89	1.21	1.43	1.55
Aluminium cans	0.02	0.07	0.11	0.20	0.34
Glass	2.3	3.1	3.92	4.55	4.6

There has been a steady increase in the amounts of glass and aluminium and steel cans recycled per capita. The weight of aluminium cans collected increased fifteenfold from 1,200 tonnes in 1989 to 19,600 tonnes in 1993. The number of steel can banks increased fivefold from 189 in 1989 to 1,108 in 1993, with the weight of steel cans collected from all sources increasing by 57% from just over 57,000 tonnes in 1989 to almost 90,000 tonnes in 1993. Over 250,000 tonnes of glass were collected from over 15,500 public and commercial bottle bank sites in 1993.

Source: Steel Can Recycling Information Bureau; Aluminium Can Recycling Association; British Glass Manufacturers Confederation

18. The Government's Producer Responsibility Initiative is designed to ensure that industry assumes an increased share of the responsibility for the wastes arising from the disposal of its products. The most advanced producer responsibility scheme involves the packaging industry. Using powers introduced under the Environment Act 1995 the Government will place a legal obligation on producers to take responsibility for packaging waste, and will set recovery and recycling targets to comply with the EC Directive on Packaging and Packaging Waste[166].

Energy recovery

19. Using waste to supply useful energy is a well established method of obtaining added value before final disposal, and will increasingly represent the best practicable environmental option for many wastes. Incineration in the second half of the 1990s will make much greater use of energy recovery than previously, and it is likely that many future incineration plants will be designed to generate power and heat from waste.

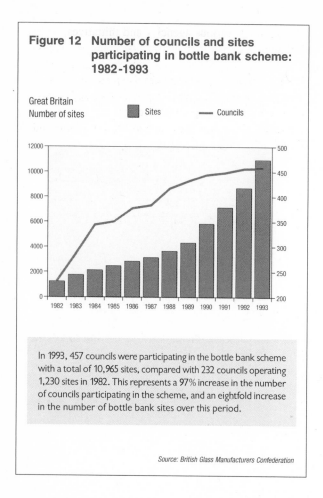

Figure 12 Number of councils and sites participating in bottle bank scheme: 1982-1993

Great Britain
Number of sites

■ Sites — Councils

In 1993, 457 councils were participating in the bottle bank scheme with a total of 10,965 sites, compared with 232 councils operating 1,230 sites in 1982. This represents a 97% increase in the number of councils participating in the scheme, and an eightfold increase in the number of bottle bank sites over this period.

Source: British Glass Manufacturers Confederation

20. The Government has set a target to recover 40% of municipal waste by the year 2005. In addition it will help to inform local communities about the potential role of incineration with energy recovery, and is providing new guidance to local authorities on the process of letting waste disposal contracts, noting the contribution that energy recovery schemes can make to sustainable waste management.

The landfill tax

21. Minimisation of waste and landfill can benefit both the environment and health, by reducing the risk of landfill gas and of leachate seeping into groundwater. Market-based instruments can produce better waste management practices in a cost effective manner, making the environmental costs explicit and ensuring that account is taken of them.

22. Consequently, the Government will introduce a landfill tax in October 1996, to reflect the environmental impact of landfill in the price paid for waste disposal. The introduction of the tax follows a programme of research and consultation by the DoE, including a report[50] in 1993 which compared the environmental impacts of landfill and incineration. There will be two rates of tax; a standard rate of £7

per tonne, and a lower rate of £2 per tonne for inactive waste which has less potential to pollute. The increased costs from the tax will be passed on to waste producers, thereby making them aware of the true costs of their activities. Such awareness will encourage less waste production, greater recovery of value from the waste that is produced (through recycling for example) and disposal of less waste in landfill sites.

23. The Government is keen to ensure that waste disposal methods are adequately policed when the new tax is introduced. The main security against fly-tipping is a strong regulatory framework. The current system of waste management licensing and the duty of care for waste provide such a framework. Further measures to prevent fly-tipping will be taken once the tax is introduced. In particular, the Environment Agencies will be asked to give a high priority to preventing fly-tipping.

Contaminated land

24. In some circumstances contaminated land can endanger health and compromise safety, such as through the escape of methane gas from uncontrolled landfill sites, the wind dispersion of asbestos debris or the presence of high concentrations of toxic substances in the ground that could be ingested. However, most land contamination is not a direct threat to health. Such land is usually the result of past industrial activities. Recent estimates of the amount of land affected in the UK vary from 50,000 to 250,000 hectares.

25. The first priority in dealing with land contamination is to prevent or minimise further pollution. A modern and effective regime for action, including criminal sanctions, has been established to deal with future pollution from contaminated land on a precautionary and preventative basis. The operation of that regime has been improved by the creation of the Environment Agencies (see Chapter 1).

25. The Environment Act 1995 introduced a new regulatory regime to deal with past pollution that has made a site a risk to health or the environment. This regime complements the existing powers under the planning system to deal with land pollution where a new use of the land is proposed. Under the new regime there will be registers of the land that local authorities identify as polluted sites, and of what has been done to reduce the contamination.

26. The Government is committed to the 'suitable for use' approach to the control and treatment of existing contaminated land. This approach requires remedial

action where the contamination poses risks to health or the environment and where suitable means of remedial action are available, taking into account the use to which the site is to be put. This supports sustainable development, both by reducing the pollution from past activities, and by permitting contaminated land to be kept in, or returned to, beneficial use wherever practicable, reducing development pressure on greenfield sites.

27. Through various agencies and initiatives, including English Partnerships, Scottish Enterprise and the Welsh Development Agency some £250 million a year of public money is spent on contaminated sites. The Government also supports research into treatment technologies for contaminated land and other initiatives such as the joint DoE and DTI Environmental Technology Best Practice Programme.

Actions: Groups 1 and 2

29. The following Group 1 and 2 actions are planned:

(1) The Government will issue guidance to local authorities to support the provisions of the framework Environment Act 1995 on contaminated land.

(2) Local authorities, in consultation with the EA, will identify and assess contaminated land within their area and secure remediation.

(3) the Government will end the disposal of sewage sludge at sea by 1998.

Actions: Group 3

30. The following Group 3 actions are planned:

(1) The Government will introduce a landfill tax in October 1996.

(2) Recycling or composting of 25% of all household waste by the year 2000.

(3) Recovery of 40% of municipal waste by the year 2005.

(4) The Government will set a target for overall waste reduction by the end of 1998.

(5) The Government will introduce regulations on the legal obligations for producer responsibility for packaging, and will set targets for waste recovery and recycling in order to comply with the EC Directive on Packaging and Packaging Waste.

3.5 Ionising and Non-Ionising Radiation[i]

Objectives

- To identify dwellings and workplaces where radon concentrations exceed the World Health Organization, WHO guidelines action level and to introduce remedial measures, with priority according to the extent to which that level is exceeded.

- To resolve the issue of safe storage and disposal of high-level nuclear waste and prevent unauthorised access to radioactive materials.

- To minimize unnecessary exposure to radiation and to ensure radiation protection at work

- To alter behaviour patterns in those European populations where sunbathing habits result in increased risks of developing skin cancer.

- To encourage informed public participation in decision-making on environmental health issues related to radiation hazards.

(EHAPE para 211)

Basis for action

Perceptions of radiation risks

> "Public perception of the risks attached to natural and man-made exposures to radiation seems to be at variance with the known facts: exposure to man-made radiation gives rise to greater concern than the normally much higher exposure to radon".
>
> (EHAPE para 206)

1. The Government is keen to ensure that public perceptions of the relative risks of exposure to radiation from various sources, and also of the relative risks from other public health hazards, do not lead to a poor allocation of public health resources. It obtains advice on radiation risks from the NRPB.

2. Studies[102] of public perception of, and attitudes to, radiation risks, including radon, have been carried out as a basis for planning publicity and encouraging public discussion. DH is currently commissioning research into public perceptions of relative radiation risks as part of it radiation protection research programme.

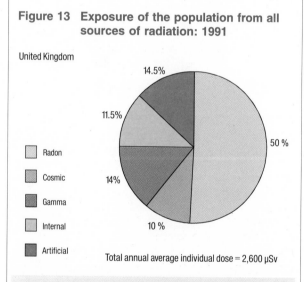

Figure 13   Exposure of the population from all sources of radiation: 1991

United Kingdom

- Radon
- Cosmic
- Gamma
- Internal
- Artificial

14.5%
11.5%
14%
50 %
10 %

Total annual average individual dose = 2,600 µSv

Some 85% of average radiation exposure of the UK population comes from natural radiation sources. Radon accounts for half of total average radiation exposure. Parts of Devon, Cornwall, Somerset, Derbyshire, Northamptonshire, Scotland and Northern Ireland have been designated **Radon Affected Areas**, because 1% or more of homes in these areas have radon levels above 10,000 µSv.

Artificial radiation accounts for almost 15% of total average radiation exposure, most of which comes from medical sources. Exposure from discharges from nuclear installations accounts for a tiny proportion (0.7%) of total exposure from artificial radiation sources.

Source: NRPB

---

[i]   Ionising radiation is so-called because it has sufficient energy to ionise material by removing electrons from atoms and molecules. Non-ionising radiation, from sunlight or power lines for example, does not have sufficient energy to trigger this process.

Radon

3. Radon is a naturally-occurring radioactive gas that is found in small quantities in rocks and soils. It can accumulate in buildings, especially in areas where the underlying ground is both permeable and contains more uranium than average. Exposure to radon increases the risk of lung cancer, and is believed to be the second most important cause of the disease after smoking. Radon also accounts for half of the UK population's average radiation dose.

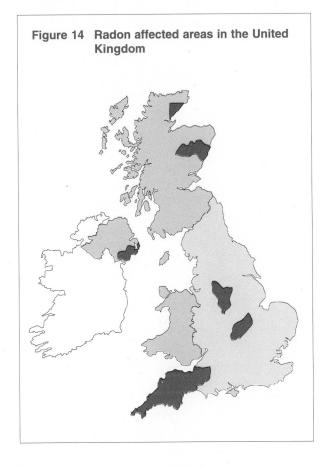

Figure 14 Radon affected areas in the United Kingdom

4. A national survey of exposure to radon in homes was carried out in the mid-1980s. This showed that average radon exposure in UK homes is low, at about 20 Bq m^{-3}, but ranges between 5 and 5000 Bq m^{-3} or more. In 1987, the Government established an Action Level for radon, above which householders are advised to take action to reduce radon entry. This Action Level was revised in 1990 to an even more stringent annual average radon concentration in air of 200 Bq m^{-3}. This is the WHO guideline action level, and is half the recommended EU action level.

5. The UK is well-advanced in identifying concentrations of dwellings that exceed the radon Action Level. Recent surveys have allowed the designation of radon Affected Areas (where at least 1% of dwellings exceed the Action Level) in England and parts of Scotland, Wales and Northern Ireland. By 1996 over 20% of the 100,000 homes estimated in 1990 to be above the radon Action Level had been identified, through the Government's free radon measurement scheme.

6. Preferred remedial methods[II] for different types of construction have also been decided upon. Guidance is available for each of these[77, 97, 98, 107], in addition to a video[105] for householders and housebuilders. Guidance[103] is also available on the Building Regulations, which ensures that the risk of new dwellings in delimited areas being above the Action Level is substantially reduced. Responsibility for remedial measures in houses rests with house-owners or the landlord in the case of both public and private rented accommodation.

7. Legislation[75] requires employers to take remedial action where workers are exposed above a defined Action Level. Where a workplace is occupied for a normal working day, the legislation is likely to apply if the radon concentration exceeds 400 Bq m^{-3} measured during the winter period. This is equivalent to the Action Level for homes, taking into account the fact that most people spend much more time in the home than at work. The Government and BRE published guidance[104] in 1995 on remedial building work to reduce radon concentrations in workplaces.

8. The Government's policy to reduce exposure to radon will focus on promoting, through publicity campaigns, remedial action by householders in homes that are above the Action Level. The results obtained from the 250,000 measurements of radon levels made in homes so far have enabled the NRPB to identify with far greater precision the areas where homes are most likely to have high radon levels. From 1 March 1996, offers of free measurements have been targeted, through personal invitations, on those householders whose homes are thought to be at greatest risk of high radon levels. Local authorities can give discretionary grants to the most needy householders to take remedial action against radon.

II   Methods include: sump systems for dwellings with solid ground floors; positive ventilation systems for dwellings with a moderate radon problem; and underfloor ventilation systems for dwellings with suspended timber floors.

Radioactive waste

9. The Government's primary aim is to ensure that radioactive waste, whatever its origin, is properly managed and that people and the environment are not exposed to unacceptable risks, either now or in the future. In July 1995, the Government published a White Paper[112] containing the final conclusions of its review of radioactive waste management policy. This took account of the responses to an earlier consultation document[113], which contained the review's preliminary conclusions. The general policy aims have been restated in the White Paper to clarify the roles of regulators, operators and Government, and to apply the concept of sustainable development. As before, it is recognised that a point can be reached where the additional costs of further reductions in risk exceed the benefits arising from the improvements in safety achieved. Safety is, and will remain, the paramount concern.

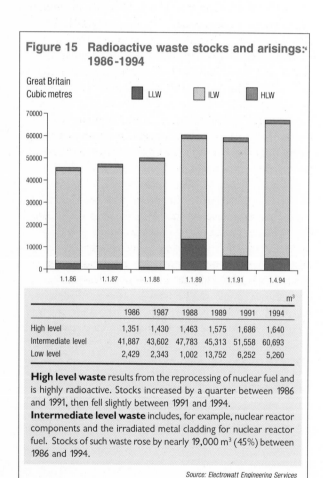

Figure 15 Radioactive waste stocks and arisings: 1986-1994

Great Britain
Cubic metres

LLW   ILW   HLW

	1986	1987	1988	1989	1991	1994
High level	1,351	1,430	1,463	1,575	1,686	1,640
Intermediate level	41,887	43,602	47,783	45,313	51,558	60,693
Low level	2,429	2,343	1,002	13,752	6,252	5,260

High level waste results from the reprocessing of nuclear fuel and is highly radioactive. Stocks increased by a quarter between 1986 and 1991, then fell slightly between 1991 and 1994.
Intermediate level waste includes, for example, nuclear reactor components and the irradiated metal cladding for nuclear reactor fuel. Stocks of such waste rose by nearly 19,000 m³ (45%) between 1986 and 1994.

Source: Electrowatt Engineering Services

10. Policy on specific issues of management of radioactive waste includes:

- a continuing commitment to the deep disposal of intermediate-level waste and support for the Nuclear Industry Radioactive Waste Executive (NIREX) programme to identify a suitable site;

- development of a research strategy for the disposal of high-level waste;

- self-sufficiency (with certain exceptions) in relation to the import and export of waste;

- acceptance of 'waste substitution' for the wastes arising from reprocessing foreign spent fuel, provided that appropriate disposal routes are available in the UK;

- five-yearly reviews of nuclear operators' strategies for decommissioning redundant plant; and

- a commitment to introduce a regime for dealing with radioactively contaminated land.

The Radioactive Waste Management Advisory Committee provides independent advice to the Government on many of these policy issues.

Electromagnetic fields

11. The NRPB Advisory Group on Non-ionising Radiation reported[37] on electromagnetic fields (EMFs) and the risk of cancer in 1992. It concluded that epidemiological findings provided no firm evidence of the existence of a carcinogenic hazard from exposure to the extremely low frequency EMFs that might be associated with living near major sources of electricity supply, the use of electrical appliances or work in the electrical, electronic and telecommunications industries. The findings of the report were endorsed by COMARE.

12. The NRPB Advisory Group published two further reports in 1993[37] and 1994[38], updating their original report in the light of further published research from Scandinavia. The second supplement concludes that the studies do not establish that exposure to EMFs is a cause of cancer but, taken together, they do provide some evidence to suggest that EMFs may be associated with childhood leukaemia. However, the number of affected children in the studies is very small.

13. The Advisory Group's reports also concluded that, to date, experimental studies have failed to establish a biologically plausible mechanism whereby carcinogenic processes can be influenced by the low levels of electromagnetic field to which the majority of people are exposed. In the absence of any convincing experimental support, the Group emphasised the need for "large and statistically robust epidemiological studies based on objective measurements of exposure to EMFs, and the need to investigate further the basis for any interaction of environmental levels of EMFs with the body"[37]. One

such study is the UK Childhood Cancer Study, which is organised by the UK Coordinating Committee for Cancer Research and partly funded by DH and SO. It is examining the possible influence of a number of agents, including EMFs, on the incidence of childhood cancer.

14. DH also provides funding to the NRPB for a programme of research into possible biological effects of electromagnetic fields from sources such as power lines and electrical equipment. The NRPB is responsible for providing advice on restricting exposure to EMFs, and has published formal guidance on protection from EMFs[37]. Neither the NRPB nor COMARE have recommended the adoption of a policy of avoidance of low levels of exposure to EMFs (higher intensities are covered by formal guidelines). This position will be kept under review.

Skin cancers

15. The incidence of skin cancer in the UK rose by about 40% in the ten years to 1988. In response, the Government has set a target for England, within the *Health of the Nation*[65] (HON) strategy, "to halt the year on year increase in the incidence of skin cancer by 2005".

16. There is usually a long interval between initial sun exposure and the development of skin cancer. Consequently, the present increase in skin cancer is unlikely to be related to increases in ultraviolet radiation caused by ozone depletion (currently estimated to be 10% in winter and spring and 5% in summer, of which only summer exposures are relevant in the UK). However, greater exposure to ultraviolet, radiation will increase the likelihood of further skin cancers, and therefore it will be important to continue taking measures internationally through the Montreal Protocol to reverse ozone depletion, in order to ensure that this does not increase the risk of skin cancers in the future.

17. The long interval between initial sun exposure and developing skin cancer also makes it difficult to monitor the effects of interventions, and to know in advance whether the HON target is likely to be achieved. Cancer registration is known to be incomplete and reporting is delayed, which means current data do not represent true incidence. The ONS will put in place new systems so that by 2005 data on skin cancer registrations should be available for the year 2003. Data on public knowledge, attitudes and behaviour will continue to be gathered through the ONS, and other research to provide information on changes in sun exposure.

18. The key to reducing the incidence of skin cancer is to reduce excessive sun exposure. Such exposure is largely determined by people's voluntary behaviour: an estimated 80% of skin cancer cases are preventable through reduction in voluntary exposure. Reducing the desirability of a tan, particularly among the young, is of vital importance in this respect. Activity in support of the HON target is under way, involving DH, the Health Education Board for Scotland, the Health Promotion Authority for Wales, the Department of Health and Social Services for Northern Ireland, the HEA, the NRPB, the NHS, commercial and professional allies and other Government Departments. Additionally, in health columns of newspapers and in women's magazines for example, the media carry information on the risk of skin cancer from ultraviolet exposure.

19. Activity to reduce skin cancer is of two complementary types: 'structural' changes (on which DH leads) to the environmental, social or economic infrastructure which give individuals choices and enable them to change their behaviour; and health education to alter attitudes in favour of less sun exposure. In the field of health education, HEA is prominent. The HEA skin cancer campaign highlights public health risks and provides information as to what one can do to avoid the hazards associated with over exposure to the sun.

Actions: Group 2

20. The following Group 2 actions are planned:

Radon

(1) The Government aims to identify at least 30,000 more homes above the Radon Action Level by the year 2000.

(2) The Government will run publicity campaigns to persuade those with homes above the Radon Action Level to take remedial action.

(3) The NRPB aims to complete research by the end of 1997 to identify the location and types of workplaces in England where radon concentrations may exceed the action level.

(4) HSE will continue to use this research at a local level to develop strategies for enforcement of radon legislation in the workplace and direct resources to workplaces at greatest risk.

Skin Cancer

In pursuit of the target "to halt the year on year increase in the incidence of skin cancer by 2005" as part of the Government's *Health of the Nation* strategy:

(5) The Government will provide information about the risk of sunburn in weather forecasts, a freephone line with information about the risks of excessive sun exposure, a personal enquiry service through the Health Information Service, and fund 'fillers' for TV and radio on the risks of skin cancer.

(6) DH will continue to fund and collaborate with the HEA in its public information activity and support for local campaign organisers, including the *Sun Know How* campaign and production of literature specially developed to reach high risk groups such as young teenagers.

(7) The NHS will continue to: run local campaigns on the risk of skin cancer; develop an 'interventions database' of successful skin cancer projects to assist local campaign organisers in designing their activities and promulgating the results; to collaborate with influential professional groups; and promote innovative ways (via the Internet for example) of influencing groups that are hard to reach.

(8) DH will continue to sponsor ONS Omnibus Surveys to measure public knowledge, attitudes and behaviour, concerning sun exposure and skin cancer.

(10) DH will commission research, worth £400,000 a year for the next four years, into the nature of skin cancer.

(11) The Government will continue to work, in collaboration with other countries and the international organisations, on phasing out substances that deplete the ozone layer.

Actions: Group 3

21. The following Group 3 actions are planned:

(1) DH and SO will continue to contribute funding for research into the possible influence of EMFs, among other agents, on the incidence of childhood cancer.

(2) DH will continue to provide funding to the NRPB for a programme of research into the effects on health of electromagnetic fields from sources such as power lines and electrical equipment.

(3) The Government will continue to develop and publish indicators of radioactivity in the environment.

(4) DH will fund research into public perceptions of relative radiation risks, the results of which are expected by 1998.

3.6 Natural Disasters and Industrial and Nuclear Accidents

Objectives

- To limit the consequences of natural disasters, prevent the occurrence and limit the consequences of major industrial and nuclear accidents, and ensure the existence of effective arrangements for emergency preparedness for and response to natural and man-made disasters, in and between countries.

- To ensure that the appropriate levels of government and the relevant public services, as well as members of the public, are fully informed of the probability and potential risks of industrial and nuclear accidents, can put those risks into perspective and understand the action required of them in the event of an emergency.

(EHAPE para 220)

Basis for action

Natural and technological disasters

1. The initial response to a disaster is usually provided by the emergency services supported by the local authority and other relevant agencies. It is at the local level that the necessary resources and expertise are found. Central government has a role in providing advice or support to the local response and in keeping Parliament informed. In a few circumstances (for example, a nuclear accident overseas) central government would be the point at which the response would start. The Home Office (HO) publication, *Dealing with Disaster*[30], and the HSE's *Arrangements for Responding to Nuclear Emergencies*[11] set out how the response to a disaster is tackled and the roles and responsibilities of the agencies involved, including central government. The HO takes the lead in providing general advice on emergency planning to the local level in England and Wales, and the Scottish Office Home Department in Scotland. The NIO takes the lead in emergency planning in Northern Ireland.

2. Local authorities and the emergency services are expected to make provision in their budgets for emergencies. There is no specific grant to local authorities to cover all emergency planning activities. In some circumstances, expenditure by local authorities is recoverable from private industry (para 9 below). Some central government assistance comes via Civil Defence grants from the Home Departments and also via Revenue Support Grant. The Environment Departments may, under the 'Bellwin Scheme' (para 3 below), provide financial assistance to local authorities in respect of response to emergencies in exceptional cases. However, this is entirely at Ministerial discretion, subject to Treasury consent, and on the basis of the financial burden of the emergency on the authority.

3. The **Bellwin Scheme** covers the costs for only certain immediate works for safeguarding life or property, or for preventing suffering or severe inconvenience. Of these costs, it covers 85% of eligible expenditure above a threshold annually reviewed by the Environment Departments: the 15% that local authorities have to meet is intended to encourage them to take a prudent financial approach to dealing with emergencies. The Bellwin Scheme was last operated for a purpose related to the environment or environmental health following an extensive fire on Thorne Moor, near Doncaster, in 1995.

Water

4. Water and sewerage companies (water supply authorities in Scotland) are required by Directions[119] to formulate plans to ensure the provision of essential water supplies and sewerage services at all times. These plans include the provision of any works, plant and equipment that is considered necessary. In ensuring the provision of potable water, companies would, as far as possible, provide the water from alternative sources. Where this is not possible from a mains supply, the company would need to have plans to bring water into the area by other means such as tankers, with distribution from bowsers placed in the street. The EA and SEPA, which have responsibility for the water environment, also have a duty under Directions[120] to ensure their essential functions are discharged at all times. Both Directions are to be updated and reissued shortly. The plans under the Directions are complementary to those for industrial installations, as described in para 7 onwards below.

5. Under the Reservoirs Act 1975, raised reservoirs with a capacity of over 25 000 cubic metres must be inspected regularly by qualified engineers appointed to a panel by the Secretary of State. A Supervising

Engineer is required to supervise the operation and maintenance of each such reservoir and report annually to its owners. An Inspecting Engineer is required, at intervals not exceeding ten years, to report on the condition of each such reservoir and advise on measures which must be carried out by the owner in the interest of public safety and on other measures which it may be in the interest of the owner to perform. Local authorities are currently responsible for enforcement of these provisions and have reserve powers to carry out works in the interest of public safety if the owners fail to do so. For some reservoirs, emergency plans have been prepared.

6. Emergency procedures to deal with flooding by rivers or from the sea involve a number of bodies, including the EA and the SEPA, police and local authorities. In England and Wales, the EA in partnership with the police and local authorities ensures that plans are in place for disseminating flood warnings to the public, businesses and statutory bodies. Local authorities and the emergency services take action as outlined in *Dealing with Disaster*[30]. SEPA issues flood warnings and has a statutory duty to advise councils, in their role as planning authorities, on flood risk.

Industrial major accident hazards

7. The UK has a well established system of controls aimed at preventing industrial major accident hazards and limiting the consequences to humans and the environment of any that do occur. In 1984, the UK implemented the Seveso Directive[167] with *The Control of Industrial Major Accident Hazards Regulations 1984*[25] (CIMAH), which have since been amended three times. The legislation is based on the following principles:

> - the *identification* of major hazards through a requirement on sites to notify authorities where certain dangerous substances are stored or handled in excess of defined quantities;
>
> - the *prevention* of major accidents by a requirement on operators to demonstrate safe operation by showing that they have identified major accident hazards and taken adequate steps to prevent them, and for the most hazardous sites, a requirement to submit to the authorities a detailed written report on their activities; and
>
> - the *mitigation* of major hazards by a requirement on operators to produce on-site emergency plans and on local authorities to produce off-site emergency plans.

This legislation is enforced by the HSE.

8. The legislation requires those responsible for certain industrial chemical establishments to identify the risk of accidents occurring and to demonstrate the safety of their operations. There are stricter requirements for potentially more hazardous installations, including duties to submit written safety reports, prepare on-site emergency plans, and to provide sufficient information to people who live or work near the premises on what to do and how they would be warned.

9. Local authorities also have powers and duties under the CIMAH Regulations: they must prepare off-site emergency plans, for which they can charge; they administer a statutory planning consent mechanism to control the storage or use of hazardous substances at existing or new establishments; and, through land-use planning policy, they ensure that risks to people are taken account of in planning decisions on new developments in the vicinity of major hazard installations.

10. This framework of controls is supported by guidance advising industry on what they should do, and by a programme of systematic inspection of sites by HSE inspectors to assess compliance with the law. Further support is provided by ensuring that health and environmental protection is effectively incorporated into emergency plans by means of exercises, regular reviews and promoting effective communication between responsible organisations.

Response to chemical incidents

11. Within the UK, plans are in place at all levels, including central and local government, health authorities and major industry, for the emergency response to accidents in which, for example as a result of fire or spillage, chemicals are released to environmental media. Such plans cover not only domestic accidents but also accidents overseas. The plans specify the organisational arrangements and make provision for informing the public. The plans cover not only the immediate response by emergency services but also the health care of those affected and clean up. These plans are regularly tested in exercises.

12. In the event of an incident, there are three principal sources of advice and assistance:

> - the National Poisons Information Service is available 24 hours a day, 365 days a year and, on request, provides health-care staff with information on the toxicity of chemicals and the diagnosis, treatment and management of people who have, or may have, been exposed;

- the Health Advisory Group on Chemical Contamination Incidents is available, in the event of a major accident, to provide wider advice on public health risk assessment, care of those affected, and follow up action; and

- a National Chemicals Emergency Centre, based at the Atomic Energy Authority's Culham Laboratory, and part funded by the DoE, provides a 24-hour information and advisory service on chemicals. This is widely used by emergency services dealing with incidents involving chemicals.

13. Further work is needed to develop and inform the public health response to chemical accidents – especially in the context of risk assessment, the rapid availability of expert information and advice to those dealing with the incident at the local level, and consideration of the need for follow up action.

14. Legislation implemented on 11 April, 1996 has improved the framework of controls over pipelines carrying dangerous substances on and off-shore. The legislation aims to ensure the integrity of pipes through goal setting requirements. This allows for different approaches from operators and give much needed flexibility to enable advantage to be taken of new technology or improved knowledge about risk.

Transboundary effects

15. Existing legislation, administrative and enforcement mechanisms achieve the aims and standards of protection required in the United Nations Economic Commission for Europe (UNECE) Convention on the Transboundary Effects of Industrial Accidents. The UK, along with all other members of the EU, is unable to ratify this Convention until a proposed Directive to replace 82/501/EEC is adopted.

16. The UK supports this proposed Directive which will clarify existing controls, improve enforcement of controls throughout Europe, and introduce new provisions such as land use planning to improve protection of human health and the environment from the effects of industrial chemical accidents.

New European directive

17. The UK is participating in the framing of a new European directive which will build on existing law to improve further the major hazard controls that exist across the EU. The main additional benefits which this will bring are:

- an increased emphasis on *managerial/organisational issues* by a requirement on operators to produce a major accident prevention policy which will set out the arrangements for risk management;

- more reliance on *generic categories of substances* (eg flammable, toxic) to determine application of the directive instead of using long lists of named substances, leading to much greater flexibility in dealing with the changing pattern of dangerous substance usage;

- *improved emergency planning* arrangements by a requirement on authorities to test plans at routine intervals;

- *more consistency* in approaches to the implementation of major hazard controls between Member States.

18. The new regime is expected to come into force in 1998. The UK is confident that this framework will provide a sound basis for the prevention of major accident hazards for the foreseeable future. There are costs associated with the regime: on companies in preparing safety reports, producing on-site emergency plans and providing information to people living and working in the vicinity of installations; and on local authorities in preparing and testing off-site emergency plans. The precise costs and benefits are difficult to quantify but the benefits of a rigorous control strategy are likely to far outweigh the costs. Major accidents are invariably costly, both directly and indirectly as a result of the loss of public confidence.

Nuclear accidents

19. Within the EU, nuclear matters are dealt with under the Euratom Treaty. Nuclear emergency response is also covered by international arrangements set up under the auspices of the International Atomic Energy Agency. The UK also has bilateral early notification arrangements with a number of other Governments.

20. The transport of all civil radioactive materials within the UK is subject to regulations based on the recommendations of the International Atomic Energy Agency. The main principle behind the regulations is that safety is built into the package design which must protect transport workers and the public from the hazards of radiation *under all foreseeable circumstances*. Safety features in the packaging are graded according to the quantity and nature of the

radioactive contents to ensure that the potential for release is small, even under severe accident conditions.

21. Nevertheless, emergency plans are in place to cover incidents involving radioactive materials under all modes of transport. The principal responsibility for emergency planning rests with the consignors, and the nuclear industry has produced plans which cover transport accidents over the whole UK and its territorial waters. The main plans are the Irradiated Fuel Transport Flask Emergency Plan, and the Nuclear Industry Road Emergency Plan. These plans are complemented by National Arrangements for Incidents Involving Radioactivity.

22. There are well established plans and arrangements for dealing with the consequences of an accident at a UK civil nuclear site. Prudence dictates that such plans should be prepared, although the chances of any accident happening which could have consequences for members of the public are very remote.

23. The arrangements follow the normal principles for emergency response in the UK. The initial reaction would be at the local level, and would be handled, as appropriate, by the site operator and the local agencies. These local agencies (which include the police, local authority and fire service) are involved in the preparation of emergency plans to protect the population which could be affected in the event of a radiological emergency and the testing of plans at regular intervals in exercises. Representatives of relevant Government Departments are also involved in this process. The Agricultural Departments have a specific responsibility for the food chain which is particularly vulnerable in the event of a nuclear accident.

24. The Government's role in an emergency would be to brief Parliament, the media and the public at the national level; and coordinate the provision of any necessary specialist assistance or extra resources needed to support the local response. The Government would also appoint an independent technical adviser, called a Government Technical Adviser, to provide advice to the local emergency services on the action they should take to protect the public. At media briefings, the Government Technical Adviser would also be the authoritative Government spokesman on the course of the emergency.

25. The supply of information to members of the public who could be affected by a nuclear emergency is governed by the Public Information for Radiation Emergencies Regulations (PIRER)[101], which are supported by a guide[60]. The regulations implement European Commission, EC Directive 89/618/Euratom[158]. PIRER requires that members of the public who live close to a nuclear facility and are at risk from a reasonably foreseeable radiation emergency should receive certain prescribed information in advance of any emergency happening. This information is distributed at regular intervals and is also permanently available to the public. PIRER also requires local authorities to prepare and keep up-to-date arrangements which ensure that members of the public actually affected by any nuclear emergency receive prompt and appropriate information covering the facts of the emergency and advice on intended health protection measures.

26. The duration and extent of an emergency would depend on the scale and nature of the radioactive release. Once the release had ended, environmental contamination would be checked and anyone who had been evacuated would be advised by the police when they could return home. At about this stage the emergency condition would be officially terminated, but the return to completely normal conditions might take place over a period of time.

27. Broadly similar arrangements are in hand to respond to any accident involving defence nuclear assets.

28. Following the Chernobyl accident, the UK Government also established a new plan – the National Response Plan – for dealing with the consequences of overseas nuclear accidents. A key feature of this plan was the establishment of a new national radiation and nuclear emergency response system known as RIMNET (Radioactive Incident Monitoring Network). The National Response Plan arrangements make full provision for the distribution of information concerning the effects of any overseas nuclear accident on the UK and the action required to deal with them. Such information would be issued to appropriate levels of national and local government and those engaged in the response, as well as members of the public.

29. The UK provisions for dealing with both domestic and overseas nuclear accidents have been set out in published documents[11, 82].

Other international cooperation

30. The UK recognises the importance of international co-operation in this field and will continue to play a full and active role in the work of relevant organisations. Chief amongst these are:

- the permanent Network of National Correspondents meets with the EC to examine, discuss and coordinate all initiatives taken in the field of civil protection at EU level;

– the Committee of Competent Authorities of the EU and its technical working groups which are looking at key aspects of the control of major accidents with a view to producing guidance to assist member states and industry;

– the OECD's Expert Group on Chemical Accidents which provides a forum for the exchange of information and develops common principles, procedures and policy guidance on accident prevention, preparedness and response;

– the UN's Awareness and Preparedness for Emergencies at Local Level (APELL) programme which aims to improve awareness of major hazards, in particular the response to incidents, by publishing guidance, providing training and the exchange of information through workshops, and providing technical expertise at the request of governments;

– the UNECE which has produced a Convention on the Transboundary Effects of Industrial Accidents, the signatories of which meet to share information and develop mechanisms for improving co-operation, for example, setting up a centre for emergency training and exercises;

– the International Labour Organisation (ILO) which has produced a Convention concerning the prevention of major industrial accidents;

– the UK participates in the EU, dealing with implementation of the early notification and mutual assistance schemes for nuclear accidents, including the EU Urgent Radiological Information Exchange System; and

– the UK also participates in the international nuclear emergency response exercises organised by the Nuclear Energy Agency for the OECD to test international emergency response communication systems.

Actions: Group 3

31. The following Group 3 actions are planned:

(1) All emergency plans will be tested (with the involvement of relevant services) and reviewed regularly.

(2) In February 1996, the UK let a research contract, to report by February 1997, to develop a methodology to assess accurately the risks to the environment of chemical industrial accidents.

(3) Within 18 months of the report in (2) above, the UK will promulgate new guidance on assessment of the risks to the environment from major industrial accidents.

(4) In 1998, when the Seveso 2 (COMAH) Directive is implemented, the UK will introduce new legislation. New guidance to explain the legislation will be published before the regulations are implemented.

(5) The HSE is reviewing what, if any, legislation is required for off-site emergency planning for civil nuclear sites. The review will be completed by the end of 1996.

(6) Through its international involvement, the UK will seek to ensure that there is effective international exchange of information between countries on dealing with major accident hazards; and to develop sound guiding principles.

3.7 Noise

Objective

- To reduce exposure to noise pollution that presents a significant threat to health, well-being and quality of life.

Note: EHAPE does not specify an objective for noise. The above is a UK objective.

Basis for action

Noise and health

1. Noise is perhaps the most widespread of pollutants. It affects the quality of life and, for some people, destroys it entirely. Excessive noise can have a wide variety of effects ranging from annoyance, increased stress and loss of sleep, to permanent damage to hearing. However, the links between noise pollution and health are not always clear cut. Whilst it is clear that prolonged exposure to very loud noise can cause permanent hearing damage, the relationship between other types of noise and ill health is complicated by various factors, including the sensitivity of the recipient.

2. A major survey[36] of attitudes to noise was carried out in 1990; one in three of those interviewed said that environmental noise spoiled their home life to some extent. The survey also found that road traffic noise is the most widespread form of noise disturbance, and that people object most to neighbour noise. Annoyance, anger, anxiety and resentment are the most frequently reported personal consequences of exposure to noise in the home. Neighbour noise continues to be a major concern, with complaints to local authorities still rising steeply.

The Government's policy

3. The Government's aim is to minimise noise pollution in all its forms, in order to improve local environmental quality and reduce the health risks posed by excessive noise. It aims to achieve this by:

- quantifying and assessing noise problems;

- promoting and encouraging the reduction of noise at source; and

- enabling local authorities to provide effective remedies for noise sufferers.

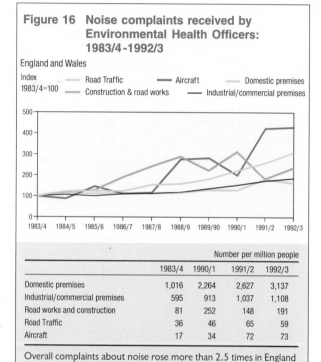

Figure 16 Noise complaints received by Environmental Health Officers: 1983/4 - 1992/3

England and Wales

Index 1983/4=100

Road Traffic — Aircraft — Domestic premises
Construction & road works — Industrial/commercial premises

	1983/4	1990/1	1991/2	1992/3
Domestic premises	1,016	2,264	2,627	3,137
Industrial/commercial premises	595	913	1,037	1,108
Road works and construction	81	252	148	191
Road Traffic	36	46	65	59
Aircraft	17	34	72	73

Number per million people

Overall complaints about noise rose more than 2.5 times in England and Wales between 1983/4 and 1992/3. Domestic premises are the largest source of complaints about noise, accounting for two thirds of all complaints in 1992/3. Between 1983/4 and 1992/3 complaints about noise from domestic premises more than trebled.
Increasing numbers of noise complaints do not necessarily mean an increase in actual noise levels but may reflect an increasing propensity for people to complain about noise.

Source: CIEH, REHIS

4. In order to monitor the incidence of noise complaints, and conduct research on the significance and characteristics of noise problems, the DoE consults extensively with other Government Departments, CIEH and a number of professional and voluntary groups concerned with environmental noise issues.

Regulation

5. There are a number of ways of tackling noise at source and preventing it from becoming a problem. For example, there are strict health and safety regulations to protect those exposed to constant high levels of noise at work (see section 4.2). Noise emissions from a wide variety of products, including vehicles and mechanical equipment, are also subject to progressive reduction through regulation (see section 5.3). The Building Regulations specify sound insulation standards to help prevent noise in newly-built dwellings and property converted after 1992. The reasonableness of the current sound insulation standards for dwellings will continue to be monitored and consideration given to ways of improving compliance with them.

Land use planning

The land use planning system plays an important role in separating conflicting land uses and thus helping to minimise the impact of noise. *Planning Policy Guidance Note 24. Planning and Noise*[93] issued in 1994 advises local planning authorities on the issues to be considered in determining planning applications for noise sensitive and noise generating developments. The guidance recommends noise exposure levels for new dwellings close to transport and other major noise sources.

Education and informal remedies

7. Education and publicity are important in increasing awareness of the health problems caused by excessive noise. In February 1996, the National Society for Clean Air and Environmental Protection, supported by the DoE, issued a leaflet containing simple advice on ways to avoid domestic noise problems. The leaflet is being distributed by local authorities, libraries, citizens' advice bureaux and retail outlets. In addition, it is being distributed to individual households in four areas where the DoE is funding research to assess its impact.

8. A variety of informal and formal remedies exist to deal with noise problems. An informal approach between neighbours is very often the best way of resolving domestic noise problems. Mediation is another valuable option. In November 1994, the DoE issued advice[93] to local authorities encouraging mediation as a potentially powerful option in resolving neighbour noise problems.

Formal remedies

9. However, informal remedies are not always possible or successful, and local authorities and individuals have powers to formally remedy noise from any premises, including land, and certain types of noise in the street which are judged to be a statutory nuisance (*ie* prejudicial to health or a nuisance). In October 1994, an interdepartmental working party was set up to review the effectiveness of neighbour noise controls. The conclusions and recommendations of the working party were published for consultation in March 1995[83]. The Government, with the CIEH and the Association of Chief Police Officers, and their equivalent organisations in Scotland, are taking forward the proposals from the neighbour noise review to encourage improved local authority noise services and liaison between local authorities and the police, by preparing good practice guidance and a code of practice.

10. A Private Member's Bill, the Noise Bill, promotes the legislative recommendations of the review. It clarifies the current powers to temporarily confiscate noise making equipment and introduces a new night noise offence. This new offence is based on the measurement of noise against an objective standard of what would be likely to cause sleep disturbance and would confirm a serious neighbour noise problem. The suggested night time neighbour noise is based on a standard above which complaints of sleep disturbance are likely to occur. It has been proposed that the noise being complained of must exceed 35 dB $L_{Aeq, T}$ and exceed the underlying noise level by at least 10dB. It is hoped that the Bill will receive Royal Assent in the Summer.

Actions: Group 3

11. The following Group 3 actions are planned:

(1) The potential links between noise and health will be studied as part of the DoE noise research programme, to complement work being carried out by other organisations in the UK and abroad.

(2) The Environment Departments will continue to encourage the use of informal remedies to resolve a wide range of neighbour disputes through: publicity to raise awareness of neighbour noise; dissemination of

research into the cost-effectiveness of mediation; and funding of 'Mediation UK' to support new community mediation services.

(3) The Government will bring into force the power to confiscate noise-making equipment in Autumn 1996, and will introduce a new night noise offence from April 1997.

4 Living and Working Environments

4.1 Urban and Rural Settlements

Objectives

* To improve social and physical living conditions in settlements, particularly for the disadvantaged, in order to prevent disease and accidents and enhance the quality of life.

(EHAPE, para 245)

Basis for action

Housing policy

1. The priority aim of the Government's housing policy is to ensure a decent home is within reach of everyone, through promoting home ownership, securing better value for money in the public rented sector, promoting the private rented sector, and maximising the use of existing stock. In pursuing this aim the Government has regard to what the country can afford.

2. The justification for Government intervention in housing was first and foremost a health one. The impact of housing on the environment has long been recognised. Poor housing can pose obvious environmental health problems for urban and rural dwellers alike. Location, design (particularly for those with special needs) and appearance are also relevant.

Housing conditions

3. Today, as a result of considerable Government investment and action on slum clearance and housing improvement, particularly over the last fifty years, the nation enjoys vastly improved housing conditions. The 1991 *English House Condition Survey*[39], the *Scottish House Condition Survey*[117], the *Welsh House Condition Survey*[149], and the *Northern Ireland House Condition Survey*[86] all show, for example, that virtually all dwellings have a bath or shower in a separate bathroom; an inside WC; and that over four fifths of the stock has full or partial central heating (see also Section 2.1).

Changes in dwellings conditions and amenities 1971 – 1991

	1971	1981	1991
Dwellings lacking in basic amenities	16.4%	5.0%	1.0%
Dwellings lacking central heating	69.0%	43.0%	16.0%
Unfit dwellings (1969 standard)	7.5%	6.2%	4.1%

Source: English House Condition Survey

4. The housing fitness standard provides a statutory yardstick against which local authorities assess the fitness of dwellings. The standard comprises a set of minimum condition and amenity requirements (see Annex 6) deemed necessary for a dwelling to be fit for human habitation. Local authorities are required to take enforcement action against the owners of dwellings they identify as unfit. Currently an authority may decide to demolish, close or, more usually, require an owner to repair such dwellings.

5. Against the background of proposed legislative changes on private sector renewal (see para 28), the Government intends to commence a review of the fitness standard and its application before the end of 1996.

6. Judged against the fitness standard, the 1991 English House Condition Survey found around 1.5 million dwellings – or fewer than one in ten – were unfit. This represents a reduction of 10% on the equivalent 1986 figure. In Wales, unfitness fell from 19.5% to 13.4% between 1986 and 1993.

7. In Scotland, the 'Tolerable Standard' as defined in Part IV of the Housing (Scotland) Act 1987, is the only statutory measure of housing quality. In 1991, 4.7% of Scotland's occupied housing stock fell below the Tolerable Standard. Results from the 1996 Scottish House Condition Survey are due in 1997.

8. The 1991 Northern Ireland House Condition Survey[86] estimated that just over 50,300 dwellings out of a total stock of some 574,000 were unfit. Changes in Northern Ireland's housing legislation mean that a direct comparison on fitness cannot be made with earlier surveys. However, a statistical modelling exercise indicates that unfitness under the revised standard reduced from more than 11% in 1987 to 8.8% in 1991. A new survey will be carried out in 1996.

Housing problems

9. Housing conditions have therefore been improving significantly. However, this does not mean that the remaining problems will solve themselves. Within a generally satisfactory overall position, there remains a need to reduce still further the level of unfit housing – particularly in the private rented sector which has the highest incidence of unfitness and in respect of dampness and cold for which there is a growing body of evidence on the links with physical health. Dampness and cold in housing, along with factors such as overcrowding, lack of facilities for young children to play, and poor design contributing to problems of crime, noise and lack of privacy may also affect mental health – for example, through increased stress and depression. Houses in Multiple Occupation (HMOs) can present particular problems for overcrowding, fire safety and means of escape.

10. But while the links between housing and health are recognised, poor housing and poor health are typically only two of a range of problems which tend to occur together. Because the number of factors at play are often complex and interwoven it is difficult to establish whether improving poor housing will, by itself, bring corresponding improvements in health. This does not remove the need for action – this is why many of the Government's policies are directed towards tackling poor housing conditions – but clearer evidence of health benefits resulting from improved housing is needed.

Housing demand

11. Over and above health considerations, the demand for more homes – caused by more people living longer, by more people living on their own and the shift to providing care services (for example for elderly or disabled people) in the community rather than in institutions – has.to be met in a sustainable way. Housing development should not encroach unacceptably on green field sites which are part and parcel of a healthy environment. Care should be taken to ensure that new developments are sensitive to local circumstances. Better use needs to be made of our urban areas and people need to be encouraged to live and work in them.

12. Planning and land use policies are directed at making better use of derelict and empty urban land for housing; and by providing, with appropriate sensitivity, for higher density developments within towns and cities, make best use of the existing infrastructure and reduce the need for green field sites. Rural settlements are also important in sustaining a healthy and thriving rural economy (see paragraph 41 onwards).

Targeting resources

13. Through a statutory, regulatory and advisory framework central government works in close partnership with local government, housing associations and the private sector in the delivery of its housing policies. These policies aim to maximise housing choice and facilitate the levering in of private investment alongside that from the public purse to help meet individuals' aspirations. This allows both central and local government to concentrate on assisting those in real need – those who are in the poorest housing conditions and those who need help to get a decent home.

Current and future actions

14. The Government set out its proposals for housing in England and Wales in the 21st century in a Housing White Paper: *Our Future Homes – Opportunity, Choice, Responsibility*[89]. Many of the proposals in the White Paper are included in housing legislation currently being considered by Parliament. The following paragraphs set out the major areas in which Government is working to improve environmental health in urban and rural settlements.

Energy efficiency

15. The Government is committed to improving energy efficiency in new and existing homes by requiring higher building standards, promoting awareness of energy issues and through local authority targets. Comprehensive building regulations ensure that new homes are well designed and built.

Strengthened building regulations for thermal insulation and ventilation came into force in July 1995. Energy efficiency measures can be particularly effective in reducing the incidence of condensation and mould growth and in providing affordable warmth. The active promotion of energy efficiency across all sectors of the existing stock benefits environmental health and is also an important part of sustainable development.

16. The Government is also committed to improving the energy efficiency of the housing stock as part of its commitment to reduce UK CO_2 emissions to 1990 levels by the year 2000. Domestic energy currently accounts for about a quarter of UK CO_2 emissions.

17. The range of programmes and measures in place to improve and promote energy efficiency across public and private sector housing includes:

- the **Energy Efficiency Best Practice programme** which plays a technical underpinning role and has a total budget of about £17.5 million in 1996/97 (covering buildings and industry);

- the **Standard Assessment Procedure (SAP)** which has been developed by the Government as the national standard for home energy rating. SAP provides an indication of the energy efficiency of a dwelling on a scale of 1-100 – the higher the rating, the more energy efficient the property. As part of the strengthened building regulations which came into force in July 1995 (see para 15), new dwellings, including conversions, are required to have a SAP rating. The Government is working with mortgage lenders to encourage them to incorporate SAP home energy ratings and energy efficiency advice into valuation survey reports and to offer homeowners green loans or other financial services to help improve the energy efficiency of their homes;

- the **Home Energy Efficiency Scheme (HEES)** which gives grants for basic insulation and draught stripping to the homes of low income, disabled or elderly (over 60) householders. Over 1.25 million homes have been treated since the scheme began in 1991. Grant provision for 1996/97 is around £73 million;

- the **Wasting Energy Costs the Earth campaign** (WECTE) which promotes the benefits of energy efficiency to householders so that they can save money on their fuel bills and improve the comfort and warmth of

---

their homes. Government expenditure of around £10 million since 1994 has been matched by private sector support;

- the **Energy Saving Trust** which is an independent organisation set up by the Government, British Gas and the Electricity Companies to develop and manage new programmes to promote energy efficiency in domestic and small business sectors. The Trust is to receive Government funding of up to £50 million over the period 1996/97 to 1998/99. The Trust aims to use the funding to maximum advantage by stimulating further investment and promoting the development of self-sustaining markets for energy efficient goods and services; and

- the **Environmental Standard Award** is an environmental quality assessment method for new homes which uses SAP to determine the energy rating. It seeks to minimise the adverse effects of new homes on the local and global environment, while promoting a healthy indoor environment. It will help home buyers to choose homes which have less impact on the environment. Emissions of greenhouse gases, together with other issues such as sustainable or recycled materials, site ecology, efficient use of water and higher levels of comfort, must all meet the 'consensus-defined' standard to qualify.

---

18. Local authorities are expected to take full account of energy efficiency in their housing strategies and in the annual housing investment programmes they submit to Government. The Home Energy Conservation Act 1995 requires all local housing authorities to prepare and submit reports identifying measures which will lead to a significant improvement in the energy efficiency of residential accommodation across all tenures. Guidance on the Act has been issued to local authorities in England indicating that the Government regards improvements of 30% as significant and encouraging authorities to draw up strategies on a ten-year timescale.

Research and monitoring

19. The Government is committed to a continuing programme of housing research which supports both the development and evaluation of policy through studies of social and technical issues and of the economic, financial and management aspects of housing and urban regeneration. The agreed programme for 1996/97 will be announced through a

press notice with a newsletter for potential contractors. The cost of the programme for 1995/96 was £7.8 million.

20. The Government is undertaking a further English House Condition Survey in 1996 for publication in 1997. The English House Condition Survey is the principal source of information on the condition of the housing stock and is used to assist in the design and monitoring of policies directed at its repair and improvement. The Survey is conducted every five years and has four principal components. These are: the physical survey of dwellings; interview surveys of occupants; postal survey of local authorities and housing associations; and market value surveys.

Health and safety standards in houses in multiple occupation

21. The Government is strengthening local authorities' powers to ensure health and safety standards in HMOs. Provisions in the housing legislation currently before Parliament are designed to secure improved standards of health and safety in HMOs. Local authorities will be able to establish registration and control schemes to regulate conditions and will be required to check fire safety precautions in large HMOs where tenants are most at risk. HMO landlords will also be subject to a clear duty to keep their properties at the required standard and any breach of the duty will be a criminal offence.

22. In Northern Ireland, where different arrangements apply, detailed consideration will be given to how best to implement the thrust of the Government's proposals for control and enforcement of HMO standards. Any legislative changes will be made at the earliest opportunity.

Measures on homelessness

23. A key Government target is to ensure that there is no necessity for people to sleep rough. The **Rough Sleepers Initiative** (RSI) is helping to reduce the number of those sleeping rough. The Government has invested over £180 million since 1990, funding outreach and resettlement workers to help and encourage people sleeping rough to take up accommodation; hundreds of beds in temporary accommodation and 3,300 permanent homes. The latest count (November 1995) by voluntary sector agencies found around 270 people sleeping rough in central London, down from estimates of over 1,000 when the RSI began in 1990. Resources and activities in central London are targeted in five zones, for which consortia have been established, bringing together the

efforts and expertise of statutory and voluntary agencies. This approach has been an important factor in helping thousands of people to start a new life away from the streets.

24. In its strategy paper, *Rough Sleepers Initiative, the Next Challenge* [114], the Government announced proposals to continue the RSI in central London and to extend it to Bristol. Further consideration is also being given to the extent of rough sleeping and the need for Government assistance in 23 other areas in England. The Government is making £73 million available to fund the RSI from 1996/97 to 1998/99.

25. Local authorities are required under housing legislation to secure accommodation for homeless households in priority need groups (for example those with children, the vulnerable, etc). In the year ending December 1995, 120,810 households in England were accepted for permanent rehousing. The Government's proposed reform of the homelessness legislation (currently before Parliament) will require local authorities to assess all applications for social housing on the basis of their long term needs. There will continue to be a safety net for priority need groups. Local authorities will be required to ensure that suitable accommodation is available for such households for at least 24 months; this will be sufficient time for households to be allocated long-term housing.

26. There is no evidence of anyone sleeping rough in Northern Ireland. The Northern Ireland Housing Executive is required by housing legislation to secure accommodation for homeless households in priority needs groups (including persons at risk of violence and young persons at risk of sexual or financial exploitation). 4,014 households were accepted as homeless in Northern Ireland during 1994/95. The Executive has an effective strategy for dealing with homelessness and the numbers are on a downward trend.

27. In Scotland, over the years 1991-94, the SO has made available around £29m in extra capital allocations specifically for homelessness projects, including those which help roofless people, such as temporary accommodation and drop-in centres. 30,900 households were assessed as homeless or potentially homeless in 1993-94.

Private sector renewal

28. Home owners are primarily responsible for repairing and maintaining their homes. The last English House Condition Survey showed that home owners carried out £28 billion worth of work to their homes in 1991, including DIY. Most people can and

do maintain their homes to an acceptable standard. However financial assistance from public funds in the form of house renovation grants is provided where owners do not have sufficient resources to undertake repairs themselves. The grants are administered by local authorities. Since 1990, means tested renovation grants (including disabled facilities grants) have provided up to 100% support for essential repairs and improvements to the poorest home owners. Around 350,000 grants have been given in England since 1990, totalling £1 billion. £254 million is being made available for 1996/97.

29. Currently grants are mandatory for owners whose properties are identified as unfit and who meet means tested criteria. However, the demand for such grants has greatly exceeded available resources and prevented local authorities from developing local area renewal strategies which can be more effective than meeting needs as they arise.

30. It is important that available resources are spent as effectively as possible. The Government therefore intends (in housing legislation currently before Parliament) to replace mandatory house renovation grants with discretionary grants for the same purpose and introduce other changes which will strengthen the ability of local authorities to develop effective local renewal strategies. The Government will, in particular, look to local authorities to develop local renewal strategies which help to:

- improve the housing conditions of vulnerable people – especially children, disabled people and the elderly – and tackle problems such as cold and damp; and

- support community care policies and help people who are elderly, ill or disabled to continue to live independently.

31. The Northern Ireland Housing Executive's Renovation Grants Scheme broadly mirrors the scheme which operates in England and Wales. The revised grant proposals contained in the Housing Grants, Construction and Regeneration Bill are being considered to determine how they might be applied to Northern Ireland. Any legislative change will be made at the earliest opportunity. The abolition of mandatory grants, except for Disabled Facilities Grant, will allow the Executive to be flexible in targeting grant towards specific areas on a worst first basis and the means test will ensure that grant is targeted towards those in most need.

Provision of affordable housing

32. Housing Associations are the main providers of new social housing. The Government provides funding through the Housing Corporation and Housing for Wales,

which are non-departmental public bodies, and through local authorities. Public investment is providing an average of around 60,000 additional social lettings in England and 3,000 in Wales each year – in line with the latest information on housing need. These additional lettings are provided through new build and the rehabilitation of existing properties, and through incentive schemes which help social tenants to buy their own home in the private sector, thereby releasing their existing home for reletting. In Wales, the Estate Partnership scheme embraces many features of this initiative. Provision is about £11m a year.

33. The Northern Ireland Housing Executive and Registered Housing associations plan to provide more than 6,600 additional social lettings over the next three years.

Measures and programmes to regenerate run down areas

34. A holistic approach is taken to tackle run down urban and other areas in England. The following key activities are funded through the Single Regeneration Budget whose objectives include enhancing the quality of life of local people, including their health and cultural and sports opportunities; tackling crime; and improving community safety:

- **Housing Action Trusts (HATs)** are providing a radical solution for run down former council housing estates. Their statutory objectives are: to repair, improve and manage the housing they provide; to improve the living, social and environmental conditions in their areas; and to encourage diversity of home ownership and tenure, giving tenants a choice of future landlord.

- The **Estate Action** programme has helped to transform run down local authority housing estates into places where people want to live by providing extra resources to encourage local authorities to tackle the physical conditions of their estates; improve housing management; secure greater tenant involvement; provide variety and choice in housing; and create opportunities for training and enterprise. In 1994/95 expenditure was £373 million with expenditure for 1995/96 estimated at £314 million.

- **City Challenge** is helping revitalise urban neighbourhoods through partnerships between the local authority, the private and voluntary sectors and the local community. It brings about sustainable improvements in deprived areas by allocating resources in response to competitive bids from local authorities. This process has encouraged authorities to draw up imaginative, ambitious and realistic plans to revitalise key urban areas. Health improvements (for example, through the provision of new or improved health centres and facilities) are a high priority for City Challenge partnerships. Subject to satisfactory performance, the 31 partnerships will each receive £37.5 million over the five-year period 1992/93 to 1997/98.

– Funds are also allocated through the **Single Regeneration Budget Challenge Fund** for new regeneration initiatives, to encourage sustainable economic growth and protect and improve the quality of life of local people, including their health, cultural and sports opportunities. More than 150 of the 372 schemes so far approved have a significant housing content and are expected to receive funding of around £1.5 billion over their lifetime. The schemes supported under rounds 1 and 2 of the Challenge Fund should result in the construction or improvement of about 170,000 homes and are expected to deliver over their lifetime more than 500 new community health facilities. Improvements will also be made to a further 700 community health facilities. The third round of the Challenge Fund was launched in March 1996.

35. Housing is a key component of urban regeneration in Scotland. Local authorities and Scottish Homes are key partners in local regeneration strategies. The primary examples of Government urban strategy are the Urban Partnership Initiatives in which housing improvements have a key element. Already over 2,000 homes have been built and over 7,000 improved. In 1995-96, almost £12m was identified within local authorities' capital allocations for expenditure within the partnership areas, and Scottish Homes planned to spend nearly £29m there. The Partnership's multi-agency approach has been adopted more widely in areas such as the Smaller Urban Renewal Initiatives (SURIs) led by Scottish Homes. There are now 15 SURIs and by the end of 1994-95 1379 new or improved houses had been provided with the aim of a further 850 in 1995-96.

Improving local authority housing through inward private investment

36. Local authorities may transfer their housing stock to housing associations, if their tenants and the

Secretary of State agree. Such transfers bring benefits in terms of investment in the housing stock (some £3 billion of private finance has been generated for the purchase and improvement of transferred stock to date), better service, increased accountability to tenants and capital receipts for local authorities. The Government is committed to transforming, through a public and private sector partnership, the remaining large scale, poor quality, council estates by 2005. As part of the 1995 Public Expenditure Settlement a new fund – **The Estates Renewal Challenge Fund** – worth more than £300 million over the next three years, was established to facilitate the transfer of these estates, largely in urban areas, to new registered social landlords. The transfer of these estates will result in their improvement through inward private investment.

Housing management in local authority housing

37. The quality of life for people living on local authority housing estates is being improved by raising standards of housing management and giving tenants a greater say in how their estates are run. One of the key elements has been compulsory competitive tendering of housing management, involving tenants at all the key stages in the competition process. Additionally, the Government has given tenants important new legal rights, including the right:

● to take over management of their estate as part of a Tenant Management Organisation; and

● to have urgent repairs which might affect health, safety and security done quickly and easily.

38. The Government is attaching high priority to helping councils tackle vandalism, crime, and other forms of anti-social behaviour on council estates so as to make them safer and less stressful places to live. A package of measures, designed to help local authorities tackle anti-social behaviour, are included in Housing Bill now before Parliament. Local housing authorities are being encouraged to work closely with the police, health and social service authorities and other agencies to develop a strategic approach.

Tackling empty homes

39. Too many homes and flats lie empty or unused. Across England over 4% of housing is vacant – about 800,000 homes. The majority are in the private sector. The Government is supporting the Empty Homes Agency, which is helping local authorities develop empty property strategies. Tackling empty property will continue to be an important element of local

housing strategies. A key target for the next decade is to reduce the proportion of homes lying empty to 3%. Under the **Housing Partnership Fund** this year,a priority is being given to schemes that bring empty property back into use. The fund provides Government resources (£30 million in 1996/97) for innovative schemes by local authority partnerships involving local authorities, housing associations and the private sector. Government resources are supplemented by money from the private sector and other sources.

Quality and design

40. The **Quality in Town and Country Initiative** which aims to raise awareness of the importance of good design and quality both in individual buildings and in the built environment as a whole. The Initiative is not only concerned with buildings – but also with parks, open spaces and trees, traffic management, air quality and the provision and quality of services. The Government propose to issue a good practice guide on design, particularly urban design in 1997.

Rural Settlements

Rural White Papers

41. The Rural White Paper, *Rural England*[115], sets out the Government's policy on all aspects of life in rural areas. It aims to encourage action to improve the quality of life in the countryside, foster improved rural services, and to promote viable communities with a balanced composite of age, income and occupation. Scotland and Wales[130] have published their own White Papers setting out their priorities.

Rural Development Commission

42. The Rural Development Commission (RDC) is the Government's main countryside agency for diversifying the rural economy, and promoting the social welfare of its inhabitants. The RDC runs a number of programmes, some of which they design to raise the standards of living, and to ensure living in rural areas does not disadvantage individuals. The RDC forecast spend for 1996/97 is £33m (this does not include running costs, VAT and receipts), the bulk of which will be spent on rural regeneration, national advisory work, and countryside action. An example of

the kind of programme the RDC runs is the Redundant Building Grant. The grant is used to refurbish derelict buildings for use as viable business premises, thereby creating jobs, and using old buildings that have become an eyesore to the local environment.

43. Rural Challenge is another scheme administered by the RDC. This annual competition is for innovative and imaginative projects which address social and economic problems in rural areas and encourages partnerships between the private, voluntary and public sectors. There are six winners a year with each receiving up to £1m in funding.

44. The RDC also administers the Rural Transport Development Fund on behalf of the DOT. The Fund fosters public transport to assist the mobility of those without access to private transport. Such provision is important to those who need access to other services, including health facilities. The RDC will provide a total of £1.25 million during 1996/97[1].

Rural Action

45. This scheme seeks to promote community-led projects to enhance the local environment, including the tackling of dereliction and pollution. The RDC, English Nature and the Countryside Commission jointly fund it (£1.2 million a year). They offer grants of up to £2,000 towards the costs of projects, specialist advice, technical services or training. They can then meet the balance of the costs from other sources and can include donated materials or volunteers' time.

46. The Housing Corporation's rural housing programme provides new social housing in England in small rural settlements of 3,000 and less in population. Between 1989/90 and 1995/96 this rural programme has provided public funding for around 12,000 new social homes in rural areas. The target for 1996/97 is 1,500 new social homes.

47. Scotland takes the same general approach in achieving rural settlement objectives but the measures and administrative arrangements used differ to suit Scottish circumstances. Since 1989, Scottish Homes has invested over £329m in rural areas providing over 9,000 new or improved homes. In 1995-96, Scottish Homes invested over £60m to provide more than 1,700 homes.

---

[1]   For further information about the RDC contact The Rural Development Commission, Dacre House, 19 Dacre Street, London SW1H 0DH (tel: 0171 340 2900).

Actions: Group 1

48. The following Group 1 actions are planned:

   (1) continuation of the RSI in Central London and extension to Bristol. The Government is considering the extent of rough sleeping and the need for assistance in 23 other areas and is making £73 million available to fund the RSI from 1996/97 to 1998/99.

Actions: Group 2

49. The following Group 2 actions are planned:

   (1) A review of the housing fitness standard and its application to commence before the end of 1996.

   (2) Continuing Government commitment to improve energy efficiency across public and private sector housing, with a range of programmes and measures designed to achieve this. Following the Home Energy Conservation Act 1995 local authorities will prepare and submit reports to Government identifying measures which will lead to a 30% improvement in energy efficiency in residential accommodation across all tenures (paras 13 to 16), including Home Energy Efficiency Scheme with grants of £73m in 1996-97.

   (3) A continuing programme of housing research.

   (4) A further English House Condition Survey to be completed in 1996 and published in 1997.

   (5) Securing improved standards of health and safety in houses in multiple occupation.

   (6) Legislative changes to Northern Ireland's arrangements for control and enforcement of HMO standards.

   (7) Changes to give local authorities greater flexibility to develop effective strategies for private sector renewal.

   (8) Legislative changes to Northern Ireland Renovation Grants Scheme to allow effective targeting to those in greatest need.

   (9) an additional 180,000 social lettings in England and 6,600 in Northern Ireland provided over the next three years;

   (10) Continuing work by HATs on run down council estates in order to improve living and other conditions.

   (11) Revitalisation of urban neighbourhoods, including health facilities, through City Challenge partnerships between local authorities and the private sector. 31 partnerships each receiving £37.5 million over the five-year period 1992/93 to 1997/98;

   (12) Improving local authority housing by attracting inward private investment.

   (13) Bringing empty properties back into use – key target for the next decade to reduce the proportion of houses lying empty to 3%.

Actions: Group 3

50. The following Group 3 actions are planned:

   (1) Raise standards of housing management through increased competition and the new legal rights and greater say in how their estates are run that tenants have been given.

   (2) Measures to help local authorities combat anti-social behaviour.

   (3) Issuing a good practice guide on design, particularly urban design – as part of the Quality in Town and Country Initiative.

4.2 Occupational Health and Safety

Objectives

- To reduce progressively but significantly the frequency and severity of occupational accidents and diseases and narrow the disparities between countries and between high-risk and low-risk occupations, through the wider adoption of measures that are in force in the best-run workplaces.

- To establish and develop high quality, cost-effective occupational health services as an integrated and basic element of a comprehensive health strategy for the working population of the European Region.

- To ensure eventual access in all countries to a comprehensive occupational health service which reflects the risks to which workers are exposed, giving the most immediate attention to those workers who are at greatest risk of work-related disease and injury.

(EHAPE, para 254)

Basis for action

The Health and Safety Commission and the Health and Safety Executive

1. The relatively high standards of health and safety at work in the UK are built on a tradition of health and safety regulation originating early in the 19th century.

2. This tradition has culminated in a single comprehensive framework of legislation regulating virtually all the risks to health and safety arising from work activity, and working through a single integrated set of institutions. This was achieved through the Health and Safety at Work etc Act 1974, which has facilitated a comprehensive view of needs and provisions in health and safety, and coordinated action to tackle them in a way related to actual levels of risk.

3. The Act established the HSC and HSE. In response to the UK Government's Deregulation Initiative, HSC has carried out a wide-ranging review of health and safety regulation, publishing a report[111] in 1994. The review concluded that the system of regulation was widely supported but recommended that HSC continue to rationalise and modernise health and safety legislation. HSC has now embarked on a programme of legislative reform to reduce the volume of legislation and to simplify and clarify that which remains. This will improve compliance by making it easier for employers and others to understand what is required of them. This will enable them to concentrate on maintaining improving standards of health, safety and welfare at the workplace, free of unnecessary reading, form-filling and record keeping.

The principal Regulations

4. *The Workplace (Health, Safety and Welfare) Regulations 1992*[152] cover a wide range of health, safety and welfare issues and apply to most workplaces. The Regulations include goal setting standards for the provision of adequate ventilation by fresh or purified air, temperature in indoor workplaces, and lighting sufficient to allow people to work and move about safely. The Regulations also require that workplace equipment and systems be maintained in good working order.

5. The broadly goal-setting *Control of Substances Hazardous to Health (COSHH) Regulations 1994*[25] provide a framework for controlling people's exposure to hazardous substances arising from work activities. They require the employer to assess the health risks created by the work and to take action to prevent or, where it is not reasonably practicable, adequately control such exposure. The employer is also required:

> - to maintain control measures properly, and to take all reasonable steps to ensure they are used properly;
>
> - to monitor exposure of employees to hazardous substances and to carry out appropriate health surveillance, where specified by the Regulations; and
>
> - to provide employees with appropriate information, instruction and training.

6. *The Noise at Work Regulations 1989*[84] require employers to take specific action to reduce the risk of hearing loss among employees caused by loud noise at

work. The main duties include noise assessments, implementing noise control measures, informing workers about the risks to hearing, making ear protectors available, and ensuring their use. The regulations also impose certain duties on employees and on machinery makers and suppliers.

Prevention of work related ill health

7. The UK has separate systems for the prevention and treatment of work related ill health. Employers are legally responsible for prevention by means of competent management assisted by occupational health and safety advisers. Some, mainly larger, companies have access to such advice from their own, in-house, occupational health services (OHS) whilst others may be members of group OHS or make use of outside consultants. Treatment is provided by means of primary and secondary health care providers through the NHS, although some companies may also offer aspects of treatment through their OHS. In addition, under the NHS, workers have unrestricted, free access to general practitioners and specialist hospital facilities when they feel that their work may be affecting their health.

8. Risk assessment is well-established as a central principle of UK law on health and safety at work. Employers and others creating risks are legally required to assess these arising in their workplace so as to determine scientific risk reduction measures. In seeking to consolidate this approach, HSE is giving priority to making risk assessment easier to understand.

9. The UK has promoted in the EU the use of risk assessment combined with cost-benefit analysis to achieve risk reduction measures which are rational, affordable and commensurate with the risk. The UK will continue to press for greater coherence and consistency of approach and methodologies at national and international level.

Reporting of work related ill health

10. An effective health and safety regime depends critically upon sound information on work injuries, ill-health and dangerous occurrences. Prompt and accurate reporting of incidents is essential if enforcing authorities are to have proper opportunities to investigate. Aggregated statistics[69, 70] guide the development of policy and enable priorities to be set.

11. New regulations came into force on 1 April 1996 which simplify the requirements for reporting work related injuries, ill-health and dangerous occurrences

and establish a single coherent legal framework to govern such reporting across virtually all economic sectors. The new system will be extensively publicised and aims to improve the rate of reporting accidents and other events with the potential to cause harm. In addition to the data from the statutory reporting system, HSE uses data from Labour Force Surveys and the systematic recording of information from accidents which are investigated. These sources enable HSE to produce representative in-depth information for important types of accidents within and across all major economic sectors.

12. The existing occupational injury and disease reporting schemes show that, even after allowing for the shift in the number of employees working in high risk sectors to working in the service industry, the UK's performance in risk prevention and control is equal to or better than that of other developed countries. These reporting schemes and other analyses indicate a number of priority areas and problems:

- management competence;

- competent occupational health advice;

- practical solutions to health problems;

- health and safety in small and medium size enterprises (SMEs); and

- in terms of specific injuries or diseases, musculo/skeletal disorders, stress, depression, lung disease (asbestosis/asthma), hearing loss, and hand-arm vibration.

Improving performance

13. Difficulties in managing health and safety at work require specific efforts to improve workplace performance, particularly in SMEs. The UK has launched a major 3-4 year publicity and interventions campaign on managing health, which recognises that small firms often do not have management structures and systems to tackle occupational health problems. It will seek to provide them with the information they need to take necessary action themselves and to decide when to seek further advice and guidance from for example, occupational health practitioners. HSE publishes guidance[48, 54, 55, 131] on the basic process of managing health.

14. Training is the key to achieving and sustaining competence. HSC has launched an initiative to encourage more and better health and safety training, with special emphasis on small firms, management and safety representatives. Competence based qualifications for occupational health and safety practitioners are being developed - the first, in general health and safety, was launched in June 1995.

15. HSC has set as a priority a major study to determine which of their various contact techniques work best at achieving health and safety improvements by SMEs. The study, based on a standardised evaluation method, aims to identify and assess the changes in health and safety performance brought about by seminars, workshops, mailshots and publicity initiatives, as well as by inspection. The results will provide important information about the stimuli behind any changes, for example intervention by the regulatory authorities, liaison with intermediaries or the employer's own initiative.

16. HSE publishes simple, easy to use guidance on a wide range of issues and problems. Where these bear on specific risks such as those mentioned above - for which specific action programmes and targets have been set - they illustrate solutions through descriptions of recognisable, real life case studies which employers can relate to their own work place problems. HSE had published, by the end of 1995/96, clear practical guidance for small firms on 11 key areas of risk. Guidance on nine more key areas will be published by the end of 1996/97.

Lead Authority Partnership Scheme

17. Many local authorities have links with local businesses through chambers of commerce and various forums. This is exemplified by a number of initiatives targeted at small firms and activity during the first phase of HSE's *Good Health is Good Business* campaign. One method by which local authorities and businesses formalise such links is to participate in the Lead Authority Partnership Scheme. The primary aim of this scheme is to improve consistency in local authority health and safety enforcement of multiple branch employers, but additional benefits include improving the partner companies' management of health and safety, and giving both partners better understanding of the other's activities.

18. There are currently 54 partnerships registered with the local authority unit. The companies involved cover most of the sectors where local authorities are responsible for enforcement and include large national companies and smaller regional based companies. The aim is to have 60 partnerships by the end of 1996/97.

19. Local authorities may have limited contact with professionals in occupational hygiene as, apart from the large retail companies and major financial institutions, many of them will be employed in the sector where HSE is responsible for enforcement.

Actions: Group 3

20. The following new Group 3 actions are planned:

(1) HSE has commissioned research on the valuation of benefits of health and safety control. The project began in September 1995 and will run for three and a half years, reporting in February 1999.

(2) HSC will issue a consultative document in 1996 on the repeal of outdated training regulations.

(3) HSE will produce an interim report in October 1996 on its study of effective techniques for helping small firms to take action proportionate to risks.

(4) By the end of 1996/97, HSE will publish the clear practical guidance for small firms on the nine remaining key areas of risk. By the end of 1997, HSE will have completed a review of all guidance it has issued.

21. In addition, HSE will continue to:

(1) Carry out audits to develop improvements in health and safety management in larger organisations.

(2) Contribute to improving the validity of international comparisons of accident and ill-health data.

(3) Further its training policy through its annual budget of £500 000 for its Training Initiative.

5 Economic Sectors

The legislation that governs all facets of the economy in regard to environmental health has been described in terms of environmental health management tools in Chapter 2, and in terms of specific environmental hazards in Chapter 3. To avoid repetition, this chapter deals only with matters which have not arisen earlier. However, the following sections are also of particular relevance to this chapter on Economic Sectors:

2.3   Control measures;

2.4   Economic and fiscal instruments; and

4.2   Occupational health and safety.

5.1 Industry

Objectives

- To define government-set goals for protecting the environment as clearly as possible, and to explicitly include requirements for health. In moving towards these goals, to take action only when careful and authoritative risk assessments and cost-benefit analyses justify it.

- Generally to install the environmentally soundest technology in all industries, having due regard to its cost-benefit and cost-effectiveness ratios.

- At all stages of industrial development, to give due attention to total quality management and continuous improvement of the quality of all aspects of industrial activity, including occupational health and safety and environmental health.

- To apply economic incentives to encourage compliance with environmental legislation, which should be carefully devised to ensure the continued modernization of the most competitive and important industries through the application of the best available technology. Decisions should be made about the scale and types of incentive best suited to encourage the phasing out of obsolescent and non-competitive industries in conformity with existing domestic competition rules.

- To use economic incentives to encourage potential investors in countries in transition, for example by limiting investors' liability for existing levels of pollution. Prior to any investment, a detailed standardized report will need to be made of existing levels of pollution on the site and its surroundings, and a timetable drawn up so that investors can reduce levels of pollution over a reasonable period of time. This approach will provide a framework on which to base environmental investments while ensuring a decrease in levels of pollution.

(EHAPE para 273)

Basis for action

Encouraging a voluntary approach by industry

1. It is central to the Government's policy towards industry that firms should be encouraged to view the environment as a business issue which should feature at the heart of their commercial strategies. The Government has therefore welcomed and nurtured voluntary efforts by industry to exceed the minimum levels of environmental performance that are established by regulation. The Government has also welcomed collective actions which enable industry itself to take the lead in meeting environmental challenges, and thus obviate the need for regulation. The Government subscribes to the principle of 'the polluter pays', and its policies on environmental protection and sustainable development support this principle.

The 'Responsible Care' programme

2. A clear indicator of industry's willingness to take voluntary action has been the increasing tendency for Trade Associations to take environmental initiatives. One of the earliest and most important of these developments is the 'Responsible Care' programme of the Chemical Industries Association (CIA). This is a voluntary initiative to respond to the public's concern about making, handling and using chemicals. The Responsible Care 'Guiding Principles' require member companies of the CIA to deliver continual improvements in health, safety and environmental protection performance and to communicate this performance to all stakeholders.

3. Indicators of performance are maintained locally by companies and at national level by the CIA. It is a condition of CIA membership that companies adhere to the Responsible Care principles. Every organisation is required to make publicly available a plain but comprehensive health, safety and environment policy statement, signed by a senior manager, which is capable of being verified. Guidance has been produced by the CIA on how to structure management systems to set and deliver Responsible Care targets. A Responsible Care regional cell network has also been set up by the CIA to encourage the sharing of best practice to SMES in the chemical industry and to neighbouring non-chemical manufacturers. The CIA is also looking to extend the Responsible Care programme through the signing of partnership agreements with allied trade associations.

Other industry initiatives

4. The CIA are not alone. There have been initiatives by a number of other trade associations. The Knitting Industries Federation has set up a working party to offer advice on environmental issues affecting the dyeing and finishing processes. The British Apparel and Textile Confederation and the Metal Finishing Association have working groups to raise awareness of environmental issues and increase the commitment to deal with them. The UK Offshore Operators Association has formulated guidelines on good environmental management and the British Cable Makers Confederation have instituted a code of practice on environmental issues. The British Leather Confederation have started a process of education and debate with their members on the best technological solution to environmental problems. The Government has welcomed these initiatives.

The Environmental Technology Best Practice Programme

5. The Government has established an Environmental Technology Best Practice Programme (ETBPP) to promote the use of better environmental practices which reduce costs for industry and commerce. The ETBPP concentrates on two main themes, waste minimisation and cost-effective cleaner technology. Within these themes the ETBPP focuses on areas of special attention where there is particular scope for it to have an impact. There are currently nine such areas, eight related to industrial sectors (for example foundries) and one to a class of pollutant (VOC). The ETBPP works with Trade associations as far as possible, and makes use of other intermediaries such as Business Links.

6. The ETBPP operates an Environmental Helpline[1], providing free advice and information to businesses on a wide range of environmental issues. The ETBPP has a particular focus on SMEs, and for companies with fewer than 250 employees the Helpline can in suitable cases arrange a short environmental counselling visit. In these cases a specialist from the Helpline's panel of environmental professionals visits the company's site and provides half a day's advice, free of charge, including a practical follow-up report.

The British Environmental Management Systems Standard

7. The British Standard (BS) on Environmental Management Systems, BS 7750, is the world's first published specification for an environmental management system. It was developed by industry itself and can be applied to any site or organisation, and to any sector. The standard is designed to enable any organisation to establish an effective management system as a basis for both sound environmental performance and participation in environmental auditing schemes. It has been produced with the express intention that its requirements should be compatible with those of the environmental management system specified in the EU's Eco-management and Audit Scheme (EMAS).

8. Applying the standard will establish a culture within businesses of analysing their environmental impacts and formulating policies and targets to tackle those impacts in line with their business objectives. The standard will encourage companies to take a methodical approach to waste minimisation, improve

---

[1] The Environmental Technology Best Practice Programme 0800 585794.

pollution control beyond the statutory minimum, and exploit recycling opportunities. Companies using the standard will enter into a process of continual improvement based on a cycle of audit and management review.

9. Trade associations are trying, with Government encouragement, to help firms in applying BS 7750, by drawing up sector application guides which will assist firms in dealing with the specific issues raised in applying the standard in their industry. There is a growing interest within the industrial community to attain BS 7750. There are now more than 120 UK companies on the register, and almost 20 overseas companies also registered to the BS. This interest in BS 7750 is probably the most obvious indicator that firms are taking a proactive stance on environmental issues.

10. The standard remains voluntary because it involves companies in going beyond the basic requirements which are covered by legislation. The competitive advantages available to companies which implement the standard are powerful factors in encouraging firms to adopt it. For example, financial savings can be made through waste minimisation and energy efficiency, and the improvement in management control and general business planning techniques. There is growing pressure on companies from customers at home and abroad to adopt positive environmental management, and those who do not may find it increasingly difficult to win contracts as specifications become tougher.

The EU Eco-Management and Audit Scheme

11. The EU EMAS goes one stage beyond BS 7750 in requiring an independently verified public statement on environmental performance. UK companies are well placed to participate in the scheme because of UK industry's interest in environment management and the fact that certification to BS 7750 should meet all but the reporting obligations of EMAS. The Government welcomes the increasing interest in positive environmental management and is promoting the benefits of registration to the EMAS scheme.

12. EMAS is based on the premise that there is benefit to companies in reporting on their environmental performance, over and above the benefits to them of developing environmental management systems. The publication of an environmental statement delivers market-place advantages at many levels (for example, with customers, the media, insurers and investors), whilst EMAS registration itself brings recognition throughout Europe. The Government supports such openness and

is encouraging companies to look at the potential for obtaining competitive edge by making their environmental achievements known to customers, investors and employees. The UK is one of the leading countries in terms of the number of corporate environmental reports that are issued.

13. A new grant scheme for smaller companies (SCEEMAS) has also been introduced. SCEEMAS encourages small firms to look at the environmental impact of their business, by providing 50% of the costs of hiring experts to advise on how to establish an appropriate environmental management system and have it verified and registered under EMAS. In Northern Ireland financial assistance is available under the Environmental Management Support Scheme to encourage industry to develop environmental management systems. The scheme is similar in principle to SCEEMAS operated in England, Wales and Scotland.

The Producer Responsibility Initiative

14. The Producer Responsibility Initiative, which was launched in 1993, challenged various sectors of industry to take more responsibility for recovering value from their products when they become waste. For example, the packaging chain was asked to develop a plan to enable the UK to meet the recovery and recycling targets contained in EC Directive 94/62/EC on Packaging and Packaging Waste[168]. The Producer Responsibility Group, comprising representatives of 28 leading companies in the packaging chain, published its plan, *Real Value from Packaging Waste*[108], in November 1994.

15. Other dialogues between industry representatives and DTI/DoE officials are taking place with the following sectors: newspapers, consumer and automotive batteries, tyres, vehicles and electrical and electronic equipment. These sectors have set up working groups or consortiums and produced reports and action plans. SMEs are normally represented on these groups by their trade associations.

The Queen's Award for Environmental Achievement

16. Companies that can demonstrate significant advances in the development of products, technology or processes, which are both commercially successful and offer major benefits to the environment, may be eligible to win the Queen's Award for Environmental Achievement. These prestigious awards were established in 1993, and sit alongside the annual Queen's Awards for Export and Technological

Achievement. Winners have ranged from multi-nationals to SMEs, across a wide range of industrial sectors. The Awards attract considerable media coverage and the winners are announced in a special supplement to the London Gazette on the Queen's birthday, 21 April. In 1996 six awards were made. All recipients of the Award are profiled in the Queen's Awards Magazine which is published annually. By providing high profile examples of commercially successful and environmentally beneficial initiatives by companies of all sizes, the Awards help to encourage others throughout industry to follow suit.

The Advisory Committee on Business and the Environment

17. In the 1990 Environment White Paper, *This Common Inheritance*[138], the Government undertook to establish a forum to promote general dialogue with business on environmental issues. The Advisory Committee on Business and the Environment (ACBE) was established in May 1991 to fulfil this commitment. Its terms of reference are: to provide for dialogue between Government and business on environmental issues; to help mobilise the business community in demonstrating good environmental practice and management, building on existing initiatives and activities; and to provide a link with international business initiatives on the environment. The committee's members are all senior business leaders, drawn from some of Britain's top companies across a range of sectors.

18. The Government places considerable value on the input ACBE makes to policy-making. Following successful terms under the Chairmanship of Sir John Collins, head of Shell, and Derek Wanless, Group Chief Executive of National Westminster Bank, the Committee has now been reconstituted under the chairmanship of David Davies, Chairman of Johnson Matthey plc.

Actions: Group 3

19. The following Group 3 actions are planned:

(1) The Government will continue to encourage the extension throughout industry of initiatives similar to the Responsible Care programme.

(2) The Government will continue to promote better environmental practices in industry through the ETBPP.

(3) The Government will encourage more businesses to adopt BS 7750.

(4) The Government will continue to promote the benefits of registration to the EU EMAS.

(5) The Government, in partnership with industry, will seek to extend the Producer Responsibility Initiative to include: newspapers, consumer and automotive batteries, tyres, vehicles and electrical and electronic equipment.

5.2 Energy

Objectives

- To control emissions of fossil fuel pollutants from large industrial sources (including power and heating plants, metal smelters) in those industrialized areas where health is affected by the resulting air pollution.

- To carry out environmental health impact assessment prior to making new investments in energy technologies, thereby emphasizing the need for prevention rather than subsequent mitigation.

- To reduce transboundary acid deposition and greenhouse gas emissions. In western Europe, technology is already being applied to reduce emissions of particulates and sulphur dioxide. However, if gas emissions are to be curbed further improvements in fuel efficiency will be needed, as well as much greater efforts to promote energy conservation.

- Effective pollution abatement technology is already available, but the cost of installing it in established or obsolete enterprises is prohibitive, especially during economic recession. Moreover, the initial capital will only be recovered in the medium or long term. However, other less expensive measures can be taken to reduce fuel consumption and improve energy efficiency. Discontinuing unrealistic subsidies, for example, would undoubtedly reduce fuel consumption and thereby pollution levels. However, a sudden increase in the cost of energy, especially in countries with severe winters, would involve major hardships. Changes in energy-saving policies can therefore only be achieved gradually.

- To encourage the development of cost-effective non-polluting energy sources. The local mix of energy sources will be determined by local circumstances and require appropriate monitoring to make planning possible. In deciding on their energy policies, countries will need to consider the availability of energy resources both nationally and globally (as well as the impact of individual energy sources on the environment) and the possibilities for greater use of renewable sources and wastes for energy production.

(EHAPE para 283)

Basis for action

Energy Policy

1. The aim of the Government's energy policy is to ensure secure, diverse, and sustainable supplies of energy in the forms that people and businesses want, and at competitive prices. The Government believes that this aim will best be achieved by means of competitive energy markets working within a stable framework of law and regulation to protect health, safety, and the environment. Government policies also aim to encourage consumers to meet their needs with less energy input, through better building design and improved energy efficiency.

Competition

2. The Government's approach to energy policy is that, so far as possible, decisions should be left to markets operating in a competitive environment. Steps are being taken to increase the amount of competition: larger industrial and commercial consumers are already able to choose their suppliers of gas and electricity. After 1998, all consumers – domestic, commercial, and industrial – will have the opportunity to choose their energy supplier.

3. The former publicly-owned energy utilities have been sold into the private sector. It is for the energy companies themselves (or the promoters or developers of new energy technologies) to take decisions about technologies, investment, prices, and research and development in the context of their commercial position, and to justify their proposals in terms of environmental and health impacts. There are no general price subsidies for particular groups of consumers. However, Cold Weather Payments are made to people on Income Support to help them with additional heating costs resulting from exceptional periods of cold weather.

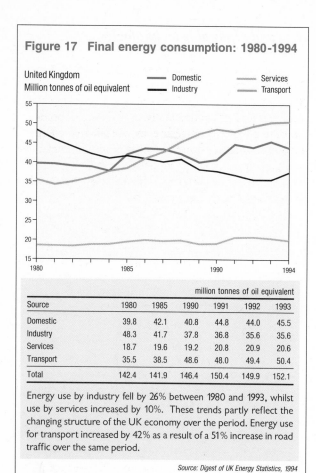

Figure 17 Final energy consumption: 1980-1994

United Kingdom
Million tonnes of oil equivalent

— Domestic   — Services
— Industry   — Transport

Source			million tonnes of oil equivalent			
	1980	1985	1990	1991	1992	1993
Domestic	39.8	42.1	40.8	44.8	44.0	45.5
Industry	48.3	41.7	37.8	36.8	35.6	35.6
Services	18.7	19.6	19.2	20.8	20.9	20.6
Transport	35.5	38.5	48.6	48.0	49.4	50.4
Total	142.4	141.9	146.4	150.4	149.9	152.1

Energy use by industry fell by 26% between 1980 and 1993, whilst use by services increased by 10%. These trends partly reflect the changing structure of the UK economy over the period. Energy use for transport increased by 42% as a result of a 51% increase in road traffic over the same period.

Source: Digest of UK Energy Statistics, 1994

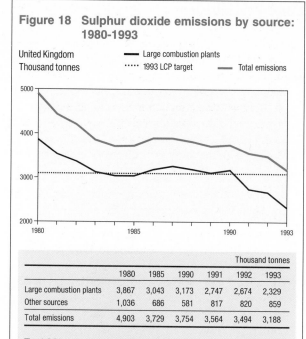

Figure 18 Sulphur dioxide emissions by source: 1980-1993

United Kingdom
Thousand tonnes

— Large combustion plants
···· 1993 LCP target
— Total emissions

				Thousand tonnes		
	1980	1985	1990	1991	1992	1993
Large combustion plants	3,867	3,043	3,173	2,747	2,674	2,329
Other sources	1,036	686	581	817	820	859
Total emissions	4,903	3,729	3,754	3,564	3,494	3,188

Total SO_2 emissions have fallen by 1.7 million tonnes (35%) since 1980. The EC Large Combustion Plants (LCP) Directive, required a 40% reduction by 1993 in annual SO_2 emissions from LCPs against a 1980 baseline. The UK achieved this with emissions in 1993 of around 2.33 million tonnes compared with the target of 3.09 million tonnes. The subsequent LCP targets required to be met are: 2.32 million tonnes by 1998 and 1.55 million tonnes by 2003.

Source: NETCEN

Regulation

4. The Government ensures, through its comprehensive systems of pollution controls (see Section 2.3) and environmental impact assessment, that each energy technology installation is effectively regulated in terms of its environmental health impact. Although the Government has no direct role in particular decisions by the supply side, companies must formulate their own plans in the context of the framework of law and regulation mentioned above. This means that companies have to comply with environmental and planning requirements. Such requirements will vary from those that are necessary to meet the UK's international commitments (such as those on CO_2, SO_2, NOx, and VOCs – see Section 3.2) to issues of local planning. The major responsibility for negotiating and promulgating these requirements lies with DoE. Enforcement is a matter principally for the EA or local authorities, depending on the issue under consideration.

5. The Government also ensures, through the Building Regulations for the conservation of fuel and power, that new buildings and those being altered are provided with cost-effective fabric insulation and space heating and hot water system controls.

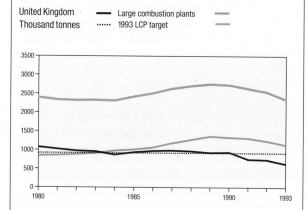

Figure 19 Nitrogen oxides emissions by source: 1980-1993

United Kingdom
Thousand tonnes

— Large combustion plants
···· 1993 LCP target

				Thousand tonnes		
	1980	1985	1990	1991	1992	1993
Large combustion plants	1,076	937	933	749	742	636
Road transport	850	1,014	1,336	1,319	1,245	1,144
Other sources	469	469	462	564	557	567
Total emissions	2,395	2,420	2,731	2,632	2,544	2,347

The EC Large Combustion Plants (LCP) Directive required a 15% reduction by 1993 in annual NO_x emissions from LCPs against a 1980 baseline. The UK achieved this with NO_x emissions in 1993 of around 636,000 tonnes compared with the LCP target of 915,000 tonnes. The LCP target to be met by 1998 is 753,000 tonnes.

Source: NETCEN

Control of emissions

6. The UK signed the UNECE Second Sulphur Protocol in 1994. This sets the UK targets for reducing SO_2 emissions from all sources by 50% by 2000, 70% by 2005 and by 80% by 2010, compared with 1980 levels. Targets for the reduction of acid emissions from existing large scale combustion plant have been set under the EC Large Combustion Plant Directive[159], and in line with the Sulphur Protocol, as follows:

- to reduce sulphur dioxide emissions by 20% by 1993, 40% by 1998 and 60% by 2003, based on 1980 levels; and

- to reduce oxides of nitrogen by 15% by 1993 and 30% by 1998, compared to 1980 levels.

7. All combustion plants require authorisations under the Environmental Protection Act 1990. These are periodically updated in the light of developing technology to ensure that the requirement to use BATNEEC is met. In granting authorisations to new combustion plant, the relevant regulatory authorities assess proposals to ensure that they are based on use of BATNEEC and an assessment of the BPEO. They also ensure that such plants do not exceed the specified emission limits in respect of SO_2, NOx and dust, laid down in the Large Combustion Plant Directive.

Nuclear power

8. The Government currently owns three major nuclear power generating companies, Nuclear Electric ltd and Scottish Nuclear ltd (which together make up the British Energy Group) and Magnox Electric plc. British Energy, which in total owns eight nuclear power stations, is being privatised. The Government will retain sole ownership of Magnox Electric, which has six operating Magnox type power stations. The companies will all continue to operate within the current stringent regulatory and safety regime.

9. The Government has placed a Non-Fossil Fuel Obligation on suppliers of electricity, requiring them to contract for specified amounts of electricity from non-fossil sources (nuclear and renewables), with the premium costs of this electricity being recovered through a levy on electricity sales. Most of this electricity comes from nuclear sources. The element of the levy that is attributable to Nuclear Electric plc will cease at privatisation, subject to the collection of any outstanding monies.

New and renewable technologies

10. It is the Government's policy to stimulate the development of new and renewable energy sources, wherever they have prospects of being economically attractive and environmentally acceptable, in order to contribute to: diverse, secure and sustainable energy supplies; a reduction in the emission of pollutants; and encouragement of internationally competitive industries. The Government will work towards 1500 MW of new electricity generating capacity from renewable sources for the UK by the year 2000. In so doing, the Government will take account of what influences business competitiveness. It estimates that electricity generated from renewable sources currently avoids the production of 750-1000 grams of CO_2 and 10-13 grams of SO_2 per kWh generated.

Clean coal technologies

11. The widespread adoption of clean coal technologies is the only realistic option to reduce the environmental impact of the forecast substantial increase in world coal use over the next decade and beyond. The Government is supporting a programme of research with UK industry and universities into advanced, cleaner coal combustion and gasification technologies which have potential for widespread take up in the medium to longer term, both in the UK and overseas. Some of the results of completed research has already contributed to reducing NOx emissions in the UK and further reductions are possible if current research is successful. The research has also contributed to the development of low NOx burners and other components which have substantial export markets as well as offering cleaner technology solutions in both the UK and overseas.

Energy Efficiency

12. The Government promotes increased efficiency in the use and supply of energy, both domestically (see Section 4.1) and in industry, for example through promotion of CHP technology. The UK is on target to meet the Government's CHP target of 5000 MW by the end of the year 2000. The current CHP total is around 3,500 MW on about 1,300 sites.

13. Incineration is an effective way of recovering energy from waste (see also Section 3.4). Where this is combined with electrical power generation and district heating it can be very energy efficient. There will be greater emphasis on energy recovery in future and it is likely that all mass burn incinerators will be designed to generate electricity and/or heat.

14. The Government is also encouraging the development of the energy services market, whereby private energy companies offer a package of energy-related services including energy efficiency measures, rather than simply selling fuel and electricity. The Government believes that cost-effective energy efficiency measures lead to improvements in economic efficiency, help to protect the environment and health through the containment of CO_2 emissions and other pollutants, and makes an important contribution to sustainable development.

Actions: Group 2

15. The following Group 2 actions are planned:

(1) Meet the UK's targets under the UNECE Second Sulphur Protocol for reducing sulphur dioxide emissions from all sources by 50% by the year 2000, 70% by 2005, and 80% by 2010, compared with 1980 levels.

(2) Reduce sulphur dioxide emissions from large scale combustion plants by 40% by 1998 and 60% by 2003, in line with the EC Large Combustion Plant Directive.

(3) Reduce oxides of nitrogen emissions from large scale combustion plants by 30% by 1998, in line with the EC Large Combustion Plant Directive.

(4) In granting authorisations to new combustion plant continue to ensure that proposals are based on use of BATNEEC and an assessment of BPEO.

Actions: Group 3

15. The following Group 3 actions are planned:

(1) Enable all consumers, commercial, industrial and domestic to choose their energy supplier by 1998.

(2) Sell into private ownership the advanced gas-cooled reactor and pressurised water reactor nuclear power stations in 1996.

(3) Encourage development of renewable energy technologies, such as solar, wind, wave and geo-thermal heat, through the non-fossil fuel obligation where it is economically attractive and environmentally acceptable to do so.

(4) Achieve the target of energy savings of 695 billion KWh per year, worth £800 million per year, by the year 2000, through the Energy Efficiency Best Practice Programme.

(5) Encourage local authorities to seek an overall improvement of 30% in residential energy efficiency.

(6) Insulate 400,000 homes under the Home Energy Efficiency Scheme in 1996-97.

(7) Continue to work, with the Combined Heat and Power Association, towards the target of 5000 Megawatts of installed CHP capacity by the year 2000, and promote CHP wherever it is economic.

(8) Continue to promote, jointly with industry and the Energy Saving Trust, measures which encourage more efficient energy use, particularly cavity wall insulation, condensing boilers and space heating controls.

(9) Continue to contribute to funding the Energy Saving Trust until the gas and electricity markets are fully liberalised.

(10) Continue to keep under review the standards in the Building Regulations for the conservation of fuel and power.

5.3 Transport

Objectives Environmental Health Action Plan for Europe

- To reduce road traffic injuries, disabilities and deaths by 25% by 2000 compared to 1990.

- To reduce gaseous and particulate emissions from road traffic to achieve levels consistent with the currently accepted air quality guidelines throughout the Region.

- To abate noise from traffic and congestion.

- To set and enforce speed limits and carry out frequent blood-alcohol tests on drivers, with appropriate penalties for those exceeding agreed levels. The rules should apply to all categories of drivers.

- To check the roadworthiness of all vehicles, including government and military vehicles and heavy goods vehicles, at regular intervals; to check at the same time their exhaust emissions and noise levels. Manufacturers or vehicle owners should be given a strict deadline to put the fault right.

- To safeguard the rights of pedestrians (especially old people, children and disabled people) by ensuring that road crossings are provided and clearly marked at frequent intervals and that pedestrians' priority on them is carefully observed; to keep pavements free from parked vehicles; to indicate clearly the sites where and times when motor vehicles must give way to pedestrians (who should in turn respect the rights of other road users); to provide bicycle lanes wherever possible and encourage their safe use.

- To regulate traffic in order to reduce accidents, pollution and noise, and to improve communications with cities by making environmentally friendly transport modes, eg, public transport and cycling, attractive alternatives. These might include, when necessary, restrictions on private and commercial traffic within the city centre and the relocation of traffic and transport streams by eg the construction of ring roads and redesign of public transport means and routes. The increasing use of heavy goods vehicles in international transport calls for cooperation between neighbouring countries to develop an integrated transport policy (see paragraph 338).

- To thoroughly investigate car accidents, at least on a suitable sampling basis, to identify the relative contributions of human, mechanical, structural and environmental (particularly road) factors to their causation; and to assess the likely impact on road safety of improvements in vehicle and road design.

(EHAPE para 288)

Basis for action

The transport system and health

1. An effective transport system is an essential part of modern life. People's jobs, their way of living, and national competitiveness in international trade depend on a modern transport infrastructure. Demand for transport in the UK is much greater than it was 40 years ago. Passenger mileage by all modes of passenger transport[I] has tripled, and the total volume of freight[II] moved has more than doubled. Road remains the dominant form of transport with 94% of all passenger mileage and 65% of freight moved in 1994.

2. But road transport has also exacted heavy human costs through the number of victims of road accidents; it was responsible for 3,621 road deaths in 1995 and more than 300,000 injuries. These figures represent significant reductions[III] on previous years which will help the UK to meet its target, set in 1987 and more stringent than the first objective above, of a one third reduction in road casualties by the year 2000 compared with the annual average from 1981 to 1985.

[I]   Car, van, taxi, bus and coach, motor cycle, pedal cycle, rail and air.

[II] Tonne kilometres of freight moved by road, rail, water and pipeline.

[III] Road accident deaths in 1995 were 35% below the 1981-1985 baseline, serious injuries 39% below, slight injuries 8% above, and overall casualties 4% below the baseline.

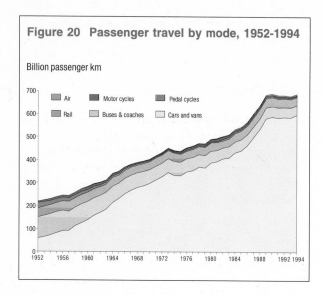

Figure 20 Passenger travel by mode, 1952-1994

Billion passenger km

Legend: Air, Rail, Motor cycles, Buses & coaches, Pedal cycles, Cars and vans

expected, notwithstanding the predicted increase in road traffic. The EC has recently published yet further proposals for vehicle and fuel standards for the year 2000 and beyond. The Government will use this opportunity to press for a cost-effective set of measures which will make further substantial progress towards meeting the air quality standards set out in the National Air Quality Strategy (see Section 3.2).

Air quality

3. Road transport is also a major source of pollution, responsible nationally for 91% of carbon monoxide (CO), 52% of black smoke, 51% of emissions of NOx and 45% of VOCs.

4. Considerable progress has already been made in reducing air pollution from transport through the introduction of improved vehicle emission standards. The first round of the latest cycle of improvements, introduced in 1993/94 for all vehicle types, substantially reduced emission limits for NOx, CO, hydrocarbons (HC), and particulates (PM) for cars, commercial vehicles and trucks and buses. These measures have effectively ensured that all new petrol-engined cars and vans are fitted with catalytic converters, which typically reduce emissions by 75-80%. Diesel vehicles have also been subjected to a particulate limit. There are already almost five million cars and vans fitted with catalytic converters – a quarter of the fleet – and natural replacement will see the bulk of the remainder fitted with them by the year 2000.

5. Nevertheless, further measures will be taken. The second round of tighter emissions standards is being introduced during 1996/97. These further requirements, which are in line with those currently being implemented in the United States, will reduce the particulate limit by 50% for heavy diesels and 43% for diesel cars, reduce the carbon monoxide limit by 19% for petrol cars and 63% for diesel cars, and reduce the hydrocarbons and NOx limits by 48% for petrol cars and 17% for diesel cars.

6. As the current fleet is replaced over the next decade by new vehicles that meet these standards, substantial reductions in road traffic emissions are

Noise (see also section 3.7)

7. Improvements in design have also brought about significant reductions in the level of noise emitted by new cars and lorries compared with their equivalents of 10 years ago. Further reductions in noise levels are to be introduced in 1996. The insulation of dwellings against noise from the construction or use of new or altered roads is the subject of regulations under the Land Compensation Acts. Noise barriers may be built alongside new roads to reduce levels of exposure to noise. Traffic management measures that are designed to slow traffic can also help to reduce road traffic noise levels.

8. Research into body rattle from heavy lorries is being undertaken and the EC is considering controls on tyre noise. Research is also continuing on various types of quieter road surface, assessing their safety and durability as well as noise benefits. Noise emissions from railway rolling stock and aircraft are also being progressively reduced as technology develops. Noise barriers are being provided in London and the South East alongside existing railway lines which have suffered intensification of use due to Channel Tunnel traffic. Older and noisier jet aircraft are to be phased out by 2002. Some airports increase landing charges for aircraft which exceed certain noise levels.

Transport safety

9. The great majority of transport casualties are the result of road accidents and the number of casualties in other transport modes is relatively small (see Figure 21). Comprehensive road accident data are collected by the Police for every incident in which a person is reported as injured. These data are collated and published each year by the ONS. Detailed analysis of these statistics, together with specific research projects, guides the development of the Government's policy on road safety.

10. DOT has already carried out considerable research over many years into the causes of road traffic accidents. The results support the view that the majority of accidents are caused by human error. The

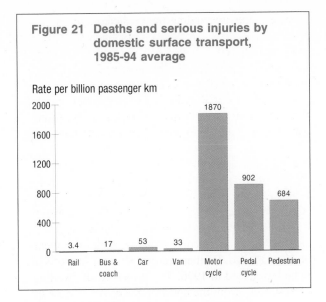

Figure 21 Deaths and serious injuries by domestic surface transport, 1985-94 average

Rate per billion passenger km

Rail	3.4
Bus & coach	17
Car	53
Van	33
Motor cycle	1870
Pedal cycle	902
Pedestrian	684

fact that only a small proportion result from mechanical defects is considered to be due to a combination of improvements in technology and in standards of vehicle and component design, and also as a result of periodical roadworthiness testing and roadside enforcement.

11. DOT runs a substantial research programme which helps to develop new standards of design, both with a view to improving road safety and tightening controls on vehicle emissions. DOT's Vehicle Inspectorate also collects information continuously on poor vehicle design and faulty components from accident investigation work and other sources. This information is used in negotiations with vehicle manufacturers over safety campaigns to recall faulty vehicles, and to shape standards for the future.

12. Almost all vehicle types have been subject to annual roadworthiness testing for many years. Vehicles which pass the test (the 'MOT') are issued with a roadworthiness test certificate to confirm that fact, and this is valid for one year. It is illegal to use a vehicle that is subject to testing without a valid test certificate. This means that a vehicle owner or operator must have faults rectified, and that the vehicle must subsequently pass a roadworthiness test, before it can legally be used on the road again. Motorists who fail to comply with this requirement are liable to prosecution and a fine of up to £1,000.

13. HSE has regulatory responsibility for ensuring that railway operators meet satisfactory safety standards, including acceptance of a 'safety case'. This document, prepared by the operators, is intended to show that effective safety management systems and measures to control risk are in place. Safety standards in both shipping and aviation are dominated by international agreements. DOT or, in the case of aviation the Civil Aviation Authority, is responsible

for translating these agreements into UK legislation and enforcing them.

Improving driving behaviour

14. It is a criminal offence to drive or attempt to drive with alcohol in excess of the legal limit (80 milligrammes of alcohol in 100 millilitres of blood) or to drive when unfit through drink or drugs. Being in charge of a vehicle in such conditions is also a lesser criminal offence.

15. For 1996-97 about £7 million has also been allocated to publicity on road safety. Included in this are the successful high profile anti-drinking and driving publicity campaigns which have been held for many years at Christmas and in the Summer. The number of fatal and serious casualties in road accidents involving illegal levels of alcohol fell by around 60% between 1983 and 1994.

16. Persuading drivers through publicity and education to drive more safely is an important element in the DOT's strategy. From 1 July 1996, the driving test has included a separate written theory test which is expected to make a significant contribution to the safety awareness of new drivers. Road safety education and training in Great Britain is largely the responsibility of local government (DoENI in Northern Ireland). An important element of DOT's road safety research programme is the devising and assessment of measures to promote safer behaviour on our roads. For example, work is being done on drink-driving, speed, young or inexperienced drivers, and safety for pedestrians and children.

Traffic management

17. The Government's transport strategy aims to strike the right balance between assisting economic development, protecting the environment and sustaining the quality of life. It recognises that public transport plays a valuable role in safeguarding the environment. For this reason spending plans have been re-focused on public transport and on more efficient use of the existing road network. The Government has welcomed moves by transport operators to coordinate services in response to demand and the creation of cross-modal strategic transport studies by a number of local authorities.

18. The Government is keen to see more freight transferred from the roads to the railways and inland waterways and provides grants to encourage this. Rail is best suited to moving large volumes of bulk material, usually over long distances. The Government

believes that the best opportunity for growth in rail freight will come from the longer distance combined rail and road traffic that is now possible through the Channel Tunnel. Measures were accordingly introduced in March 1994 to encourage this. These included a special weight allowance for lorries carrying freight to and from rail terminals, an improved grant scheme to help the development of rail freight facilities, and a grant scheme to assist with rail track charges.

19. The UK is paying increasing attention to the interaction between transport and land use planning. The Government is using the planning system to help reduce the need to travel. Planning Policy Guidance (PPG13)[91] and Planning Guidance (Wales) Planning Policy[90] (PG(W)PP) encourage local planning authorities to plan land use and transport together in ways which enable people to carry out their everyday activities with less need to travel. This could reduce reliance on the private car and make a contribution to the environmental goals set out in the Government's Sustainable Development Strategy[133].

20. PPG13 and PG(W)PP also advise local authorities to foster forms of development which encourage walking, cycling and public transport use, thereby improving access to facilities for those without a car. It promotes traffic management as a tool which can be useful in encouraging walking and cycling, as well as improving the quality of neighbourhoods, making streets safer and reducing community severance. 20 mph zones, supported by engineering measures to make them self-enforcing, can be a highly effective means of reducing vehicle speeds and accidents in residential and commercial areas as well as creating a more pleasant and healthy environment. In 1995, DoE and DOT jointly published a *Better Practice Guide to PPG13*[14] to help users implement the lessons of PPG13. The Guide provides over 100 examples of villages, towns and cities which are turning theory into reality. In Scotland, draft National Planning Policy Guidelines on Transport and Planning[94] were published in May 1996.

21. Local measures to improve transport planning and traffic management are likely to have a significant role to play in many local air quality action plans. Therefore, the Government is developing guidance on how to link air quality and land use planning considerations, as well as on the connections between traffic management and air quality (see Section 3.2).

22. The Government encourages local authorities to develop integrated and balanced transport strategies for urban areas through the 'package' approach which emphasises demand management and support for alternatives to the private car. DOT is supporting 53

such local packages in 1996-97, and has allocated £79 million to minor schemes (those costing less than £2 million) in these packages. The Government is also providing funding for the construction of the Midland Metro and will help fund the Croydon Tramlink.

23. The Government's national road construction and improvement programme also makes a valuable contribution to reducing the level of road casualties and pollution. About one third of schemes in the current programme are bypasses which are designed to remove heavy traffic from residential and shopping streets. Bypasses can bring benefits in terms of both safety and amenity to local communities. However, they may also be detrimental to the adjacent natural environment. Careful analysis of the advantages and disadvantages – in public health, environmental protection and preservation, and economic terms – is an essential part of any proposal for a bypass.

Cycling and walking

24. Cycling is widely acknowledged to be capable of conferring notable health benefits. Regular exercise through cycling can reduce mortality and morbidity from cardiovascular disease and improve weight control, skeletal fitness, strength, mobility and mental health. This is as true of utility journeys – to work, school, shop and so on – as it is of trips made for sporting, recreational or tourism purposes. Increases in cycling, if at the expense of car use, can also contribute to reduction of air pollution, particularly since cycling often replaces short car journeys which do not reap the benefit of a fully functioning catalytic converter.

25. A national strategy for cycling will be launched in July 1996. This will be based around the proposal from the Government's steering group on cycling for a target of doubling the existing level of cycle use by the year 2002. Strong encouragement is being given to measures which give people the confidence to cycle more. These include: the provision of safe and convenient cycle routes; cycle tracks with protected crossings of major traffic routes; better interchange arrangements with public transport; improved cycle parking in public places; reasonable amenities at the workplace such as showers, changing-rooms and storage lockers; and presentation of cycling as a sensible means of making a wide range of local journeys.

26. The SO published a cycling policy booklet *Cycling into the Future*[30] in April 1996 and has established a National Cycling Forum involving representatives of the new Councils, tourism and enterprise bodies and organisations with an interest in

increased cycling as a transport mode and leisure pastime.

27. The Government is also supporting the development of a National Cycle Network. The Network is being promoted by the traffic engineering charity Sustrans with Millenium Commission funding and the backing of local authorities and industry.

28. Walking also provides beneficial exercise and can help reduce air pollution when it replaces some of the many short car journeys. Government guidance on planning and transport[91] encourages local authorities to make areas and developments safer and more attractive to pedestrians. Options include traffic calming, improvements to lighting and the natural environment, and provision of wider pavements and pedestrian-friendly road crossings which avoid underpasses, long waits or detours. These steps may be complemented by measures to reduce traffic, such as areas where vehicle access is restricted.

29. Highway authorities take decisions on the provision of pedestrian crossings, and technical guidance (on siting and design) is provided by DOT. DOT is currently testing two new forms of crossing: the 'TOUCAN' crossing, a shared crossing for cyclists and pedestrians to use together; and the 'PUFFIN' (Pedestrian-User-Friendly-Intelligent) which is intended to replace the Pelican crossings in the long term.

National debate on transport policy

30. In 1995, the Government stimulated a national debate on transport policy in order to encourage wider discussion of the transport issues about which choices must be made. The debate's aim was to achieve a greater level of consensus on the way forward for transport policy. *Transport: The Way Ahead*[141], published in June 1995, contained edited versions of six speeches by the then Secretary of State for Transport, Dr Mawhinney, and a series of questions on which views were sought.

31. The Government's responded to the national debate with the Green Paper *Transport: The Way Forward*[142] in April 1996, addressing the future of transport in England. The central point made in this document was that traffic growth and its impact on congestion and pollution is a major issue which must be tackled in a more strategic manner than in the past. More than twenty key measures were set out, including proposals to bring trunk road planning more closely in line with regional land use plans, and proposals to enhance the powers of local authorities to deal with traffic growth.

32. Separate documents will be published covering transport in Scotland and Wales. In Scotland, the Government mounted a series of focus group discussions involving a very wide range of interests concerned to identify key Scottish perspectives on the transport debate. Further consultations are being undertaken before publication of a Scottish document.

Actions: Group 1

33. The following Group 1 Actions are planned:

(1) Achieve the target of a one third reduction in road casualties by the year 2000 compared with the annual average from 1981 to 1985.

(2) Continue with high profile education and publicity campaigns, costing £7 million in 1996-97 on drink-driving, excessive speed and child safety, in an effort to change driver's attitudes.

(3) Continue research, costing £4.6 million in 1996-97, to find effective methods of promoting safer driving and improving road design and traffic management measures for safety.

Actions: Group 2

34. The following Group 2 actions are planned:

(1) Improve local authorities' tools to develop transport strategies aimed at reducing the need to travel and encouraging use of less polluting modes of transport.

(2) Pilot local authority enforcement of vehicle emissions testing at the roadside.

(3) Continue enforcement by the Police and the Vehicle Inspectorate of vehicle roadworthiness and emissions at the roadside; those vehicles which are visibly in poor condition will be most likely to be stopped for spot-checking.

(4) Launch a national cycling strategy in July 1996, based on the proposed target of doubling the existing level of cycle use by the year 2002, and open main segments of National Cycle Network by 2000.

(5) Improve enforcement of emissions regulations, targeting those vehicles doing most damage to the environment.

(6) Press in the EU for a cost-effective package of vehicle and fuel standards, for implementation in the year 2000, to further reduce vehicle emissions.

(7) Support the introduction into operation of the Midland Metro by 1998 and the Croydon Tramlink by 2000.

(8) Complete the London Underground Jubilee Line Extension by early 1998.

Actions: Group 3

35. The following Group 3 actions are planned:

(1) Develop environmental responsibilities in partnership with public service and other fleet operators.

(2) Provide effective guidance to the public on greener motoring.

(3) Continue research into reducing all forms of transport noise.

(4) Complete a joint DoE/DOT study to monitor implementation of PPG13.

(5) Publish documents on the future of transport in Scotland and Wales.

5.4 Agriculture

Objectives

- To reduce human exposure to risks related to agriculture and animal husbandry without compromising the primary aims of agriculture and related activities, namely the provision of adequate and safe food. To this end, the closest cooperation will need to be established between human health, veterinary, agriculture and forestry professionals.

- To widely promulgate and apply simple and understandable rules on the amount and timing of use of pesticides, particularly in fish farms, on the wider use of antibiotics in animal husbandry, and on the application of agrochemicals on agricultural crops, if necessary through the adoption of legislation, so as to protect both the farmers and consumers as well as the surface and groundwater draining the land.

- To train farmers in the use of agricultural practices that make more limited use of fertilizers and pesticides.

- To dispose or re-use animal waste and offal in such a way that pathogens are destroyed and nitrate contamination, especially of groundwater, is minimized.

- To conduct frequent and thorough inspections of intensive animal farming practices for the early detection of infections, especially by *Salmonella* and *Campylobacter*, which, without necessarily affecting the animals themselves, present a risk to the consumer.

- To improve practices in forest management to prevent serious environmental hazards to local populations and to achieve sustainability in accordance with the recommendations of the 1993 European Conference of Forestry Ministers.

- To conduct irrigation in such a way as to reduce to a minimum the risk of salinisation and of exposure to fish and rodent-borne parasites; and to identify areas and streams where such parasites are prevalent and take strict measures to avoid human infestation.

- To conduct continuous surveillance of conditions under which agricultural produce is harvested, transported and stored, in order to minimize losses of food and the possibility of its moulding in barns and silos, as well as of contamination of food by chemicals.

(EHAPE para 297)

Basis for action

1. Some risks to health from agriculture are covered in the sections on food, water pollution and waste disposal.

Pesticides

Registration and approval for use

2. It is the Government's policy that the amounts of pesticides used should be limited to the minimum necessary for the effective control of pests compatible with the protection of human health and the environment. The primary aim of pesticide regulation is to ensure that all pesticides used in this country are safe to users, consumers and the environment. Farmers and growers must comply with the Food and Environmental Protection Act 1985 and the *Control of*

Pesticides Regulations 1986 when using pesticides, as well as the *Pesticides (Maximum Residue Levels in Crops, Food and Feeding Stuffs Amendment) Regulations 1995* and other, general, health and safety legislation. Only approved pesticides can be advertised, sold, supplied, stored or used.

3. Applicants for pesticide approvals must show that their products are effective, humane and pose no unacceptable risks to human beings, non-target species or the wider environment before approval is granted. In order to do this pesticide manufacturers are required to provide a wide range of scientific data which are subjected to rigorous scrutiny by the independent experts of the Advisory Committee on Pesticides. If any evidence emerges concerning the safety of a particular product the approval of that product can be reviewed and, if necessary, restricted or revoked.

Safe use and training

4. Farmers and growers are required to follow label instructions when using pesticides and to take all reasonable precautions to protect the health of humans, creatures and the environment. Advice on how to meet these responsibilities is given in the statutory *Code of Practice for the Safe Use of Pesticides on Farms and Holdings*. The Code contains specific advice on procedures for notifying neighbours before spraying and, in particular, advice on the need to take precautions to minimise the risk of spray drift.

5. It is important that everyone involved in the use of pesticides has adequate training to ensure that pesticides are applied safely and efficiently. Certificates of Competence are already mandatory for certain users of agricultural pesticides who must hold a certificate if providing a commercial service or if born after 31 December 1964. But there may be scope for more guidance on responsible use of pesticides, fertilisers and veterinary medicines.

6. By the end of 1996, MAFF will complete an investigation of the possibilities for encouraging better targeting of pesticides. It will also examine other means of encouraging responsible pesticide use, such as Codes of Practice, leaflets and other publicity material, and through the provision of advice and guidance by non-Government bodies such as the Pesticide Forum.

Monitoring food for pesticides residues

7. Monitoring of both home-produced and imported food for pesticide residues is carried out by the Government's Working Party on Pesticide Residues. Some 2-3,000 samples are analysed each year for a wide range of pesticides. A constant surveillance monitoring programme covers dietary staples such as bread, milk and potatoes, and there are rolling annual programmes for cereals, fish, fruit and vegetables and products of animal origin. Monitoring can be extended to cover problem areas to which the UK is alerted, by developments in other countries for example. The full results of monitoring by the Working Party on Pesticide Residues are published each year and a summary of its findings every three years.

The Wildlife Incident Investigation Scheme

8. The Agriculture Departments are responsible for the Wildlife Incident Investigation Scheme (WIIS), which monitors the impact of agricultural pesticides on birds and other wildlife. The scheme is intended to alert Government to deaths arising from the normal use of pesticides as well as deterring deliberate and

illegal poisoning. Incidents of wildlife deaths arising from approved uses are rare and certainly not on a scale which suggests that such poisonings could affect population levels. Where incidents are caused by misuse or abuse of pesticides, appropriate enforcement action is taken and offenders are prosecuted whenever sufficient evidence is available.

The Pesticides Forum

9. To assist in the development of its policy on pesticides the Government has established a Pesticides Forum, which held its first meeting in May 1996. The Forum has the aim of bringing together the views of those concerned with the use and effects of pesticides, identifying their common interests and assisting in the effective dissemination of best practice, advances in technology and the results of research and development. The Forum will advise the Government on the promotion and implementation of a range of initiatives relating to the responsible use of pesticides.

Forestry

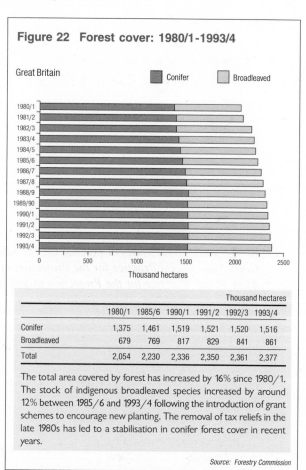

Figure 22   Forest cover: 1980/1-1993/4

Great Britain   ■ Conifer   ■ Broadleaved

Thousand hectares

	1980/1	1985/6	1990/1	1991/2	1992/3	1993/4
Conifer	1,375	1,461	1,519	1,521	1,520	1,516
Broadleaved	679	769	817	829	841	861
Total	2,054	2,230	2,336	2,350	2,361	2,377

The total area covered by forest has increased by 16% since 1980/1. The stock of indigenous broadleaved species increased by around 12% between 1985/6 and 1993/4 following the introduction of grant schemes to encourage new planting. The removal of tax reliefs in the late 1980s has led to a stabilisation in conifer forest cover in recent years.

Source: Forestry Commission

10. The Government's policies and objectives for sustainable forestry are set out in *Sustainable Forestry: The UK Programme*[134]. These policies are

based on the two principles of a steady expansion of forest cover and sustainable management of existing woodlands. To these ends, the programme sets out policies for protecting forest resources, enhancing economic value, conserving and enhancing bio-diversity and the physical environment, developing opportunities for recreational enjoyment, conserving landscape and cultural heritage, and promoting public understanding.

11. In April 1995, the Government introduced revised forestry incentives to give more emphasis to management and protection of woodlands and to encourage greater use of natural regeneration of native woodlands. A special management grant encourages woodland owners to allow the public access for recreation and exercise. The Government also supports several forestry initiatives that aim to improve urban fringe landscapes and land damaged by past industrial use and development. The National Forest in the Midlands will stimulate physical and economic regeneration in a landscape degraded by mineral extraction, and provide valuable recreational and wildlife benefits. Twelve Community Forests have similar objectives and are being established near major urban centres throughout England, in partnership with local communities.

12. Since the Ministerial Conference on the Protection of Forests in Europe held at Helsinki in 1993, the Government has published guidance on the management of native woodlands and also on the use of native species to create new woods. Planting of new broadleaved woodlands in 1994 (10,800 hectares) was greater than in any of the previous twenty years. The total area covered by forest has increased by over 16% since 1980, from 2,054,000 hectares to 2,390,000 hectares. Over the past 10 years the stock of indigenous species has increased by around 13% through new planting supported by Government incentives. New planting of broadleaf and conifer species is currently progressing at about 18,000 hectares each year. The recent Rural White Papers[115] set out the different approaches and aspiration for woodland expansion in England, Scotland and Wales.

Actions: Group 2

13. The following Group 2 actions are planned:

(1) Introduce agricultural waste handling grants in Nitrate Vulnerable Zones in 1996, once such zones have been designated.

(2) Provide free pollution advice to at least 3000 farmers and select seven river catchments for farm waste management plan campaigns in England in 1996.

(3) Use the National Farm Waste Forum to keep risks from farm wastes under review.

Actions: Group 3

14. The following Group 3 actions are planned:

(1) Revise and re-issue codes of practice on *The safe use of Pesticides on Farms and Holdings* and *A Code of Good Agricultural Practice for the Protection of Water*, and evaluate and review the *Codes of Good Agricultural Practice for the Protection of Soil and Air*.

(2) Publish research and undertake follow-up action on reduced in-put farming by the end of 1997.

(3) Investigate the development of an index of pesticide use to assess the extent to which environmental risk reduction has been achieved, and the factors affecting the adoption of techniques to reduce the environmental risk from pesticides.

(4) Continue to encourage organic farming through: promotion of the Organic Aid Scheme; support for the UK Register of Organic Food Standards; sponsorship of research into, and dissemination of information about, organic agriculture.

(5) To support with grant aid the planting of 67,000 hectares of new trees in the years 1995-98 at a cost of approximately £100 million.

(6) Approve an estimated 370,000 hectares of woodland for management grant by the end of March 1998.

5.5 Tourism

Objectives

- To ensure that the adequacy and safety of the drinking-water supply and situation facilities in resorts meet peak tourist demand. The disposal of solid and liquid waste needs to be tightly regulated, to protect beaches and shellfish beds.

- To strengthen food inspection and monitoring, particular with regard to *Campylobacter* and *Salmonella* during peak seasons, and take measures to ensure that the temporary staff hired to handle food are properly trained and that standards of personal and environmental cleanliness are observed as closely as elsewhere.

- To inform tourists immediately and objectively in the languages understood by most of them in the event of contamination of water and food or the outbreak of infectious disease, as well as in the case of water and beaches becoming unsuitable for bathing in areas they are or will be visiting.

- To strictly enforce the usual road traffic regulations in resort areas so as to reduce accidents, especially among children, to keep the quality of the air unimpaired and to prevent excessive noise.

(EHAPE para 304)

Basis for action

1. Tourism contributes some £37 billion annually to theUK economy, equivalent to 5% of the Gross Domestic Product. Like any other major service sector employer (the industry employs 1.5 million people) the tourist industry must comply with legislation on a range of issues including health and safety, food hygiene etc, which are designed to protect consumers and ensure environmental health standards.

2. The present infrastructure of services copes well, and planned improvements that are in process of implementation, such as those to water resources, distribution systems and waste water treatment, will enhance service capability.

Planning

3. *Planning Policy Guidance Note 21*[92] on Tourism outlines the economic significance of tourism and it environmental impact, and therefore its importance in land-use planning. The Government's policy is that the tourism industry should flourish in response to the market, while respecting the environment which attracts visitors but also has a far wider and enduring value. The central objective is to achieve 'sustainable development' that serves the interests of both economic growth and conservation of the environment.

Bathing waters

4. Bathing waters are monitored to ensure that they meet EC Directive Standards (see Section 3.1). The quality of some other waters is monitored in accordance with the Directive in Wales and elsewhere.

Road safety

5. The Government has allocated about £7 million for 1996-97 for publicity on road safety. This includes DOT's successful Summer anti-drinking and driving publicity campaign which has been held for many years.

Noise

6. It is the Government's policy to minimise noise pollution from all sources. To help prevent noise problems from tourism developments DoE issued planning policy guidance[92] in 1994, advising local planning authorities on how to use their powers to minimise the adverse impact of noise. The guidance advises that special consideration is required where noisy development is proposed in or near SSSIs, and where development would affect the quiet enjoyment of the National Parks, the Norfolk Broads, AONBs or Heritage Coasts. The effect of noise on the enjoyment of other areas of landscape, wildlife and historic value should also be taken into account.

7. In designated areas of the countryside and resort areas that are popular with tourists, as elsewhere, local authorities have powers to control noise nuisance from premises, including land, and certain types of noise in the street (see Section 3.7).

Caravan and camp sites

8. *Planning Policy Guidance Note 21*[92] on Tourism gives guidance on the use of land for holiday and touring caravan sites. It recognises the large numbers of people taking holidays in caravans and advises local authorities to reconcile the need to provide facilities for this with the protection and preservation of the environments which attract holidaymakers in the first place.

9. Under the Caravan Sites and Control of Development Act 1960, organisations may be exempted from the requirements for a caravan site licence (which is needed largely for public health and safety reasons) and planning permission provided that their objectives are recreational and they satisfy the Secretary of State for the Environment that they can maintain high standards of safety and conduct.

10. In Wales, the Tourist Board provides financial assistance for environmental and landscaping work to reduce the density and improve the quality of caravan and camp sites.

Fire safety

11. Hotels, hostels, boarding houses and the like are, if they are new or being extended or converted, subject to the Building Regulations. The regulations include the consideration of fire safety currently set out in *Approved Document B: Fire Safety*[9]. All but the smallest hotels and boarding houses must comply with the fire certification requirements of the local fire authority. Local authorities are responsible for licensing public entertainments with regard to provision of amenities and safety of the public in the event of fire.

12. The Building Regulations are applicable to hotels, hostels, boarding houses and other similar residential accomodation if they are newly constructed, materially altered or extended or undergo a material change of use. Guidance on satisfying the regulations with regard to fire safety is given in *Approved Document B*.

Promoting Sustainable Tourism

13. The Government is actively disseminating the principle and practice of sustainable tourism – that is tourism which can sustain local economies without damaging the environment on which it depends. Projects testing methods of dealing with the pressure of visitors at specific sites have been taking place throughout the country during the past five years. The lessons of many of these projects are examined in the document *Sustainable Rural Tourism – Opportunities for Local Action*[132], which was published jointly by the Government, the English Tourist Board and the Countryside and Rural Development Commissions in November 1995.

Actions: Group 3

14. The following Group 3 actions are planned:

(1) A revised edition of *Approved Document B: Fire Safety* will be issued for public consultation in 1996.

(2) Continue testing methods of dealing with the pressure of visitors at specific sites throughout the country in order to promote sustainable tourism which does not damage the environment.

6 International Action

The Environmental Health Action Plan for Europe

1. This chapter corresponds to Volume 3 of the EHAPE, in which WHO/EURO sets out priorities for international action in a variety of fields. Volume 3 of the EHAPE does not set out national objectives since, in general, the actions in Volume 3 are addressed to the international organisations. Accordingly, this section of the UK NEHAP describes those UK actions which are outside the normal scope of participation in international negotiation but are direct UK contributions to the WHO aims.

2. In the EHAPE, WHO/EURO defined principles and criteria for international actions which led to its choice of priority areas. The UK is making a particular contribution to some of these priority areas, as indicated below.

International cooperation

3. The UK is committed to contributing, at the European level, to initiatives for the benefit of environment and health, under the auspices of WHO/EURO, the EU, the UNECE and others.

4. At the 1994 Helsinki Conference, the UK offered to host the Third European Conference on Environment and Health to be held in 1999. That offer has since been accepted formally by WHO/EURO.

5. The MRC is playing an important part in the ESF Initiative in Environment and Health Research, following agreement at Helsinki on a regular programme of meetings between leading scientists and policy makers to produce a broad agenda of research priorities in Europe. The UK hosted the first such meeting, which took place at the IEH in Leicester in May 1995.

Support for development of action plans at country level

6. As mentioned in Chapter 1, the UK is a pilot country for the development of NEHAPs. The leader of the UK delegation was elected Chairman of the Pilot Project Steering Group and later Chairman of the NEHAPS Task Force. As a member of the Task Force the UK has contributed extensively to the NEHAPS process. The Government is also providing expert

advice to Bulgaria for the development of its NEHAP through the *Environmental Know How Fund*.

Improvement of environmental health services

7. The UK has the infrastructure and systems for providing environmental health management, and assists international co-operation in this area by exchanging information with other countries. By providing information on the UK system to nations that are developing their environmental health infrastructure, the UK helps those nations to achieve and maintain appropriate environmental health standards.

8. As well as its commitment to the EU, the Government maintains strong links and contacts at a wide international level. These include contacts at political and official levels with:

– the WHO;

– the Food and Agriculture Organization (FAO);

– the Codex Alimentarius;

– the International Standards Organization (ISO);

– the European Standards Organization (CEN); and

– the European Electrical Standardisation Organization (CENELEC).

9. The Government encourages Member States of these organisations to visit on fact-finding missions and provides information on the UK system. In addition, the UK contributes to and promotes international exchange of personnel and health professionals through such schemes as the WHO professional officer exchange and the EC 'Karlous' programme of exchanges of government officials between Member States.

Improvement of professional education and training

10. Within the UK there are long-established training institutions offering undergraduate and postgraduate qualifications for health professionals, which are overseen by the relevant professional bodies. The UK

encourages exchange of information at all educational levels, from academic exchanges to joint study tours, to provide assistance with the promotion of educational standards in other member states.

11. The CIEH and the Royal Environmental Health Institute of Scotland are founding members of the International Federation of Environmental Health, which has a wide range of membership contributing to educational projects and improvement of environmental health. There are now 20 professional organisations that are full members of the International Federation and 20 associated bodies on all five continents. These associated bodies are a mixture of academic organizations, regional groups of EHOs and groups from different countries. The CIEH is also the WHO Collaborating Centre for Environmental Health Management in Europe.

Integration of environmental health policies into economic sector policies

12. The UK has also undertaken work in response to the European Regulation EEC 93/793[153] on the evaluation and control of the risks associated with existing hazardous substances. Three official/industry working groups are producing guidance on:

- the risk assessment of existing substances;

- the technical options for risk management; and

- risk benefit analysis.

13. The DoE is also currently financing research into the applicability of a risk-benefit appraisal framework for the introduction of genetically modified organisms for environmental remediation and as a substitute for agrochemicals. The results of such projects are expected to be important in informing the EU negotiations in this area.

14. The BRE has pioneered an Environmental Assessment Method (BREEAM) to provide benchmarks and recognition for environmentally sensitive or 'green' buildings (see Section 2.3 para 25). BREEAM complements regulation and awareness programmes by establishing a market mechanism that gives a competitive advantage to buildings of higher environmental quality. Similar schemes are now under development in many other countries, internationally and within Europe, using BREEAM as a model.

Support to countries in transition

15. The UK is playing a full part in the implementation of the Environmental Action

Programme (EAP) for Central and Eastern Europe. The EAP was endorsed by the Environmental Ministerial Conference at Lucerne in 1993 as part of the UNECE's 'Environment for Europe' process, and gives priority to developing realistic, efficient and cost-effective solutions to environmental problems which threaten human health in the region. It is based on a three-pronged approach encompassing policy reform, institutional capacity-building and investment. Whilst the Programme concentrates on short-term action, it ensures that this is consistent with the longer-term process of economic, social and environmental restructuring.

16. Work on the EAP is guided by a Task Force, established at Lucerne, comprising representatives of donor and recipient governments, international organisations and financial institutions. The UK is supporting more than 200 projects of technical assistance in support of the EAP through the *Environmental Know How Fund*. UK assistance with health reform is also being provided under the Know How Fund.

Assistance to improve nuclear safety

17. Following the initiative taken at the G7 Munich Summit in 1992, the G24 countries, including the UK, have given their support to a multilateral programme of action to help the countries of central and eastern Europe and the former Soviet Union in their efforts to improve nuclear safety. This programme includes immediate measures in the areas of operational safety improvements, near-term technical improvements to plants based on safety assessments, and enhancing regulatory regimes.

18. The UK's main contribution is through EU programmes of technical assistance and the European Bank for Reconstruction and Development (EBRD) Nuclear Safety Account (NSA). The UK contributes about 16% of the EU budget, which so far has provided more than £400 million in assistance. The Government shares international concerns about nuclear safety in these countries and is keen that the UK should continue to play a full part in international assistance programmes.

European Environment and Health Committee

19. Since the Helsinki Conference, the UK has been nominated as a member of the WHO European Environmental Health Committee (EEHC), and the Government's Chief Medical Officer has been elected Chairman of that Committee for a period of two years.

Annex 1 Abbreviations and Glossary

ACMSF	Advisory Committe on the Microbiological Safety of Food
AONB	Areas of Outstanding Natural Beauty
APC	Air Pollution Control
AQMA	Air Quality Management Area
BATNEEC	Best available technique not entailing excessive cost
BPEO	Best practicable environmental option
BNFL	British Nuclear Fuels PLC
BRE	Building Research Establishment
BREEAM	BRE Environmental Assessment Method
BS	British Standard
CHP	Combined heat and power
CIEH	Chartered Institute of Environmental Health
CIMAH	Control of Industrial Major Accident Hazards
CIPFA	Chartered Institute of Public Finance and Accountancy
CMO	Chief Medical Officer
COMAH	Control of Major Accident Hazards (proposed EC directive)
COMARE	Committee on Medical Aspects of Radiation in the Environment
DH	Department of Health
DHSSNI	Department of Health and Social Services for Northern Ireland
DoE	Department of the Environment
DoENI	Department of the Environment for Northern Ireland
DPH	Director of Public Health
DTI	Department of Trade and Industry
DWI	Drinking Water Inspectorate
DOT	Department of Transport
EA	Environment Agency
EAP	Environmental Action Programme
EC	European Commission
EEA	European Environment Agency

EEHC	European Environmental Health Committee
EHAPE	Environmental Health Action Plan for Europe
EHO	Environmental Health Officer
EHRI	Environmental Health Risk Indicator
EIONET	European Information and Observation Network
EMAS	Eco-Management and Audit Scheme
EMF	Electromagnetic field
EHRI	Environmental Health Risk Indicators
ESF	European Science Foundation
EU	European Union
HAT	Housing Action Trust
HEA	Health Education Authority
HFA	Health for All
HMIP	Her Majesty's Inspectorate of Pollution
HMIPI	Her Majesty's Industrial Pollution Inspectorate
HMO	Houses in multiple occupation
HO	Home Office
HON	Health of the Nation
HSC	Health and Safety Commission
HSE	Health and Safety Executive
IID	Infectious intestinal disease
IEH	Institute for Environment and Health
IPC	Integrated pollution control
IPPC	Integrated Pollution Prevention and Control
LAAPC	Local Authority Air Pollution Control
LACOTS	Local Authority Coordinating Body on Food and Trading Standards
LEHAP	Local environmental health action plan
MAFF	Ministry of Agriculture, Fisheries and Food
MFSG	Microbiological Food Surveillance Group
MRC	Medical Research Council
NEAP	National Environmental Action Plan

NEHAP	National Environmental Health Action Plan		UN	United Nations
			UNCED	UN Conference on Environment and Development
NHS	National Health Service		UNECE	UN Economic Commission for Europe
NIO	Northern Ireland Office			
NIS	Newly independent states		VOC	Volatile organic compound
NOx	Nitrogen oxides			
NRA	National Rivers Authority		WCA	Waste collection authority
NRPB	National Radiological Protection Board		WHO/EURO	World Health Organisation European Region
OECD	Organisation for Economic Cooperation and Development		WO	Welsh Office
OFWAT	Office of Water Services		Agency	The Environment Agency for England and Wales
OHS	Occupational health services			
ONS	Office of National Statistics			
			Digest	The annual *Digest of Environmental Statistics*
PAH	Polycyclic aromatic hydrocarbon			
PCB	Polychlorinated biphenyl		Agencies	
PHCDS	Public Health Common Data Set		Environment	The Environment Agency for England and Wales, the Scottish Environment Protection Agency, and the DoE NI Environment and Heritage Service
PHLS	Public Health Laboratory Service			
R&D	Research and development			
RCEP	Royal Commission on Environmental Pollution		Departments	
			Environment	DoE, the Scottish Office Agriculture, Environment and Fisheries Department, and DoENI.
RDC	Rural Development Commission			
RIPHH	The Royal Institute of Public Health and Hygiene			
			Conference	
RPA	River Purification Authority		Helsinki	The WHO/EURO Second European Conference on Environment and Health held at Helsinki in June 1994
RSH	The Royal Society for the Promotion of Health			
RSI	Rough Sleepers Initiative		Departments	
			Home	Home Office and the Scottish Office Home Department
SAHSU	Small Area Health Statistics Unit			
SCEEMAS	Small Companies EC Eco-Management and Audit Scheme			
SCIEH	Scottish Centre for Infection and Environmental Health			
SEPA	Scottish Environment Protection Agency			
SHEPS	The Society of Health Education and Health Promotion Specialists			
SI	Statutory Instrument			
SME	Small and medium size enterprises			
SO	Scottish Office			
SOx	Sulphur oxides			
SSSI	Site of Special Scientific Interest			
SWQO	Statutory Water Quality Objective			
UK	United Kingdom			
UKAEA	UK Atomic Energy Authority			

Annex 2 References

General

1. *Advisory Committee on the Microbiological Safety of Food: Report on Campylobacter.* HMSO, 1993. ISBN 0-11-321662-9.

2. *Advisory Committee on the Microbiological Safety of Food: Report on Poultry Meat.* HMSO, 1996. ISBN 0-11-321969-5.

3. *Advisory Committee on the Microbiological Safety of Food: Report on Salmonella in Eggs.* HMSO, 1993. ISBN 0-11-321568-1.

4. *Advisory Committee on the Microbiological Safety of Food: Report on Vacuum Packaging and Associated Processes.* HMSO, 1992. ISBN 0-11-321558-4.

5. *Advisory Committee on the Microbiological Safety of Food: Report on Verocytotoxin-producing Escherichia coli.* HMSO, 1995. ISBN 0-11-321909-1.

6. *Air Pollution and Health: Understanding the Uncertainties.* MRC/IEH 1994. ISBN 1--899110-00-3.

7. *Air Quality: Meeting the Challenge.* DOE, 1995. A4954.

8. *The Application of Combined Heat and Power in the UK Health Service: Best Practice Guide 60.* Energy Efficiency Office, 1992.

9. *Approved Document B: Fire Safety.* HMSO, 1992. ISBN 0-11-752313-5.

10. *Aquatic Environment Monitoring Reports.* Occasional reports. MAFF, Directorate of Fisheries Research.

11. *Arrangements for Responding to Nuclear Emergencies.* HMSO. ISBN 0-7176-0828-X.

12. *An Assessment of Demands and Resources at 1994.* SO 1995. ISBN 0-74-807480-5.

13. *Asthma and Outdoor Air Pollution.* Committee on the Medical Effects of Air Pollutants. HMSO 1995. ISBN 0-11-321958-X.

14. *A Better Practice Guide to PPG13.* HMSO, 1995. ISBN 0-117144-8.

15. *Building regulation and health.* Raw & Hamilton, CRC, BR289, London, 1995. ISBN 1-86081-024-1.

16. *Building regulation and safety.* Cox, & O'Sullivan, CRC, BR290, London, 1995. ISBN 1-86081-027-6.

17. *British Government Panel on Sustainable Development, First Report, January 1995.* DOE, 1995. A5611.

18. *Buildings, health and safety: initial risk evaluation.* Raw, et al., Proc. Healthy Buildings '95, Milan Vol 3, 1681-1686, 1995. Available as a more comprehensive draft from BRE.

19. *The Code of Good Agricultural Practice for the Protection of Water.* MAFF WOAD 1991.

20. *Code of Good Practice on Prevention of Environmental Pollution from Agricultural Activity.* HMSO, 1991.

21. *Code of Practice on Access to Government Information (Open Government in the Department of the Environment).* DOE, 1994.

22. *Code of Practice on Food Hygiene Inspections (Code of Practice No. 9 Revised).*

23. *Code of Practice on Sludge Use in Agriculture.*

24. *The Control of Industrial Major Accident Hazards Regulations 1984, SI No. 1902.*

25. *The Control of Substances Hazardous to Health (COSSH) Regulations 1994, SI No. 3246.*

26. *Countryside Management: Water – Preventing Pollution by Nitrate.* DANI, 1994. ISBN 1-85527-116-8.

27. *Cryptosporidium in Water Supplies.* HMSO, 1990. ISBN 0-11-752322-4.

28. *Cryptosporidium in Water Supplies, Second Report.* HMSO, 1995. ISBN 0-11-753136-7.

29. *Cycling into the Future.* Scottish Office, 1996.

30. *Dealing with Disaster.* Home Office, second edition 1994. ISBN 0-11-341129-4.

31. *Declaration on Action for Environment and Health in Europe.* WHO/EURO, 1994.

32. *Digest of Environmental Statistics, No 18, 1996.* HMSO ISBN 0-11-753297-5.

33. *Drinking Water 1995: a report by the Chief Inspector, Drinking Water Inspectorate.* HMSO, 1996. ISBN 0-11-753-131-6.

34. *Drinking Water Quality in Scotland in 1993*, Scottish Office, 1994.

35. *Economic Appraisal in Central Government: A Technical Guide for Government Departments.* HM Treasury. HMSO, 1991. ISBN 0-11-560034-5

36. *Effects of Environmental Noise on People at Home – BRE Information Paper 22/93*, BRE. HMSO, 1993.

37. *Electromagnetic Fields and the Risk of Cancer.* Report of an Advisory Group on Non-Ionising Radiation: Documents of the NRPB Vol 3 (1992) No 1.

38. *Electromagnetic Fields and the Risk of Cancer*: Supplementary Report by the Advisory Group on Non-Ionising Radiation: Documents of the NRPB Vol 5 (1994) No 2.

39. *English House Condition Survey.* HMSO 1991. ISBN 0-11-752280-3.

40. *Environmental Appraisal in Government Departments.* DOE, 1994. ISBN 0-11-752915-X.

41. *Environmental Digest for Wales No. 8 1993.* WO, 1994. ISBN 0-75-040495-7.

42. *Environmental Health Action Plan for Europe.* WHO/EURO, 1994.

43. *Environmental Health Criteria 12 – Noise.* WHO, 1980.

44. *Environmental Health Risk Indicators.* DH, 1996. ISBN 0-11-753174-X.

45. *Environmental Information Regulations 1992, SI No. 3240.* (separate Regulations apply in Northern Ireland).

46. *Environment Information Strategy Review. Report of the Review on Waste Management Information.* DOE, 1995. ISBN 1-85112-205-2.

47. *Environmental Responsibility: an Agenda for Further and Higher Education.* HMSO, 1993. ISBN 0-11-27-0820-X.

48. *Essentials of Health and Safety at Work.* HSE, 1996. ISBN 0-7176-0716-X.

49. *Exposure to Radon in UK Dwellings, 1994.* GM Kendall et al, Chilton, NRPB-R272. HMSO 1994. ISBN 0-8595-1379-3

50. *Externalities from Landfill and Incineration.* HMSO, 1993. ISBN 0-11-752825-0.

51. *Fertiliser Recommendations.* MAFF, 1994. RB209.

52. *Fit for the Future: Second Progress Report on the Health of the Nation.* DH, 1995. G07/019 2792 1P.

53. *5 Steps to Risk Assessment.* HSE, 1994. Free leaflet, IND(G)163L.

54. *Five Steps to Successful Health and Safety Management.* HSE, 1994. Free leaflet, IND (G) 132L.

55. *Food Safety (General Food Hygiene) Regulations 1995, SI No 1763.*

56. *Food Safety (General Food Hygiene) Regulations (NI) 1995, SI No 360.*

57. *Fourth Report of the Independent Scientific Committee on Smoking in Public Places* ('the Froggatt Report'). Chairman: Sir Peter Froggatt. 1988 HMSO. ISBN 0-11-321131-7.

58. *A Guide to the General Food Hygiene Regulations Booklet.* DH, 1995.

59. *A Guide to the General Temperature Control Regulations.* DH, 1995.

60. *A Guide to the Public Information for Radiation Emergencies Regulations 1992.* HSE, 1992. ISBN 0-11-888350-9.

61. *A Guide to Risk Assessment and Risk Management for Environmental Protection.* DOE, 1995. HMSO. ISBN 0-11-753091-3.

62. *Health Education in Scotland – a National Policy Statement.* SO 1991. ISBN 0-11-494218-8.

63. *Health Effects of Sea Bathing (WM19021) – Phase III.* E B Pike, WrC, 1994.

64. *Health for All targets. The health policy for Europe.* WHO EURO, 1991. ISBN 0-92-8901311-7.

65. *The Health of the Nation – A Strategy for Health in England, Cm 1986.* HMSO, 1992. ISBN 0-10-119862-0.

66. *The Health of the Nation for Environmental Health.* The Institution of Environmental Health Officers, 1993. ISBN 0-900103-42-6.

67. *The Health of the Public in Northern Ireland 1994: Chief Medical Officer's Annual Report.* DHSSNI, 1995.

68. *Healthy Environments.* Welsh Health Planning Forum 1993. ISBN 0-7504-0549-X.

69. *HSC Annual Report 1994/95.* HSE Books. ISBN 0-7176-1009-8.

70. *HSC Health and Safety Statistics 1994/1995.* HSE Books, 1994. ISBN 0-7176-0852-2.

71. *IEH Assessment on Indoor Air Quality in the Home.* IEH, 1996. ISBN 1-899110-05-4.

72. *Indicators for Local Agenda 21.* Local Government Management Board, 1995.

73. *Indicators of Sustainable Development for the United Kingdom.* DOE, 1996. ISBN 0-11-753174-X.

74. *Industry Guide to Good Hygiene Practice: Catering Guide.* DH, 1995. ISBN 0-11-321-8990.

75. *Ionising Radiations Regulations 1985, SI No. 1333.*

76. *Learning for Life.* SO, 1993. ISBN 0-7480-0707-5.

77. *Major alterations and conversions: a BRE Guide to radon remedial measures in existing dwellings.* C R Scivyer 1994. BRE Guide BR250, BRE.

78. *Making Markets Work for the Environment.* HMSO, 1993. ISBN 0-11-752852-8.

79. *Making Waste Work: A strategy for sustainable waste management in England and Wales, Cmnd 3040.* HMSO 1995, ISBN 0-10-130402-1.

80. *Mediation: Benefits and Practice.* DOE, 1994 (Available free of charge).

81. *Meeting Challenges – The Housing Corporation's Priorities and Targets 1995-98.* Housing Corporation, 1995. ISBN 0-90-145458-3.

82. *The National Response Plan and Radioactive Incident Monitoring Network (RIMNET) Phase 2.* HMSO, 1993. ISBN 0-11-752788-2.

83. *Neighbour Noise Working Party. Review of the Effectiveness of Neighbour Noise Controls: Conclusions and Recommendations.* 1995. Available free of charge from DOE, SO and WO.

84. Not used.

85. *The Noise climate Around Our Homes – BRE Information Paper 21/93.* BRE. HMSO, 1993.

86. *The Northern Ireland House Condition Survey 1991.* Northern Ireland Housing Executive, 1991. ISBN 85694-018-7.

87. *On the State of the Public Health: The Annual Report of the Chief Medical Officer of the Department of Health.* HMSO, 1995. ISBN 0-11-321910-5.

88. *Our Common Future (The Brundtland Report).* Report of the World Commission on Environment and Development. Oxford University Press 1987. ISBN 0-19-282080-X.

89. *Our Future Homes – Opportunity, Choice, Responsibility.* HMSO, 1995. ISBN 0-11-129012-8.

90. *Planning Guidance (Wales) Planning Policy.* HMSO 1996. ISBN 0-7504-1839-7.

91. *Planning Policy Guidance Note 13. Transport.* HMSO 1994. ISBN 0-11-52941-9.

92. *Planning Policy Guidance Note 21. Tourism.* HMSO 1992. ISBN 0-11-752726-2.

93. *Planning Policy Guidance Note 24. Planning and Noise.* HMSO, 1994. ISBN 0-11-752924-9.

94. *Planning Policy Guidelines in Scotland on Transport and Planning.* SO 1996. ISBN 1-350-6153.

95. *Policy Appraisal and the Environment: A Guide for Government Departments.* DOE. HMSO, 1991. ISBN 0-11-752487-5.

96. *Policy Appraisal and Health: A Guide from the Department of Health.* DH, 1995. G07/032 3610 1P.

97. *Positive pressurisation: a BRE guide to radon remedial measures in existing dwellings.* R K Stephen. BRE Guide BR281, BRE 1995.

98. *Protecting dwellings with suspended timber floors: a BRE Guide to radon remedial measures in existing dwellings.* P. Welsh, P W Pye and C R Scivyer 1994. BRE Guide BR270, BRE.

99. *Public Health Common Data Set 1995. Data definitions and user guide for computer files, Volumes I and II.* Institute of Public Health, University of Surrey, 1995. Available to the NHS only.

100. *Public Health Common Data Set 1995, England.* Institute of Public Health, University of Surrey, 1996.

101. *Public Information for Radiation Emergencies Regulations 1992. SI No. 2997.*

102. *Radiation Exposure of the UK Population – 1993 Review.* Hughes, J S and O'Riordan, M C, NRPB-R263. HMSO, 1993. ISBN 0-85951-3645.

103. *Radon: guidance on protective measures for new dwellings.* Building Research Establishment 1992. BRE Guide BR211.

104. *Radon in the workplace: a guide to radon measurement and remedies for non-domestic buildings.* C R Scivyer and T J Gregory. Building Research Establishment 1995, ISBN 1-86081-040-3. BRE Guide BR293.

105. *Radon-No problem.* Video. Building Research Establishment 1994.

106. *Radon sumps: a BRE Guide to radon remedial measures in existing dwellings.* Building Research Establishment 1992. BRE Guide BR227.

107. *RCEP 12th Report: Best Practicable Environmental Option.* HMSO, 1988. ISBN 0-10-103102-5.

108. *Real Value from Packaging Waste.* 1994. VALPAK, 114 Knightsbridge, London SW1X 7LJ.

109. *A Regional Strategy for the Northern Ireland Health and Personal Social Services 1992-1997.* DHSS, Belfast, 1991.

110. *Restrictions on Human Exposure to Static and Time Varying Electromagnetic Fields and Radiation.* Documents of the NRPB, volume 4, no 5, 1993.

111. *Review of Health and Safety Regulations, Main Report.* HSC, 1994. ISBN 0-7176-0794-1.

112. *Review of Radioactive Waste Management Policy: Final Conclusions, Cm 2919.* HMSO, 1995. ISBN 0-10-129192-2.

113. *Review of Radioactive Waste Management Policy: Preliminary Conclusions.* DOE, 1994.

114. *Rough Sleepers Initiative, The Next Challenge.* DOE, 1995. ISBN

115. *Rural England, Cmnd 3016.* DOE, 1995. ISBN 0-10-130162-6.

116. *Scotland's Health – A Challenge to us All.* SO, 1992. ISBN 0-11-494218-8.

117. *The Scottish House Condition Survey 1991.* Scottish Homes, 1993. ISBN 1-874-1707-11.

118. *A Scottish Strategy for Environmental Education.* SO, 1995. Dd 84 33567.

119. *Security Measures (Water and Sewerage Undertakers) Direction 1989.* Issued by the Secretary of State under section 170, Water Act 1989 (now section 208, Water Industry Act 1991).

120. *Security Measures (National Rivers Authority) Direction 1989.* Issued by the Secretary of State under section 170, Water Act 1989 (now section 207, Water Resources Act 1991).

121. *Sludge (Use in Agriculture) Regulations 1989.* SI No. 1263 (as amended by SI No. 880, 1990).

122. *Smoking in Public Places – 2nd Survey Data.* 1996 HMSO. ISBN 0-11-753246-0.

123. *Smoking in Public Places – 2nd Survey Report.* 1996 HMSO. ISBN 0-11-752849-8.

124. *Smoking in Public Places – Guidance for owners and managers of places visited by the public.* 1992, DOE et al.

125. *Solving the Nitrate Problem – Progress in Research and Development.* MAFF, 1993.

126. *The State of the Public Health: 1994 Annual Report.* HMSO, 1995. ISBN 0-11-321910-5.

127. *Statistical Bulletin Environment Monitor for Radioactivity in Scotland 1992*. SO, 1995. ISBN 0-7480-08160.

128. *The Steering Group on Chemical Aspects of Food Surveillance – Annual Report 1994. Food Surveillance Paper No. 45*. MAFF, 1995. HMSO. ISBN 0-11-242994-7.

129. *A Strategic Guide to Combined Heat and Power*. NHS Estates, 1993.

130. *Strategic Intent and Direction for the NHS in Wales*. WO, 1989. RA395 (429).

131. *Successful Health and Safety Management*. HSE, HMSO 1991. ISBN 0-11-8859-88-9.

132. *Sustainable Rural Tourism – Opportunities for Local Action*. Countryside Commission with DNH, the English Tourist Board and the Rural Development Commission, 1995. ISBN 0-86170-464-9.

133. *Sustainable Development – The UK Strategy, Cm 2426*. HMSO, 1994. ISBN 0-10-124262-X.

134. *Sustainable Forestry – The UK Programme, Cm 2429*. HMSO, 1994. ISBN 0-10-124292-1.

135. *Sustainable Use of Soils, Cm 3165*. RCEP, 1996. ISBN 0-10-131652-6.

136. *Sustainability Indicators Research Project – Report of Consultants on the Pilot Phase*. LGMB, 1995. ISBN 0-7488-9702.

137. *Terrestrial Radioactivity Monitoring Programme (TRAMP). Annual reports*. MAFF.

138. *This Common Inheritance. Britain's Environmental Strategy. Cm 1200*. HMSO, 1990. ISBN 0-10-112002-8.

139. *This Common Inheritance: UK Annual Report 1995. Cm 2822*. HMSO, 1995. ISBN 0-10-128222-2.

140. *Towards a Healthier Environment: Managing Environmental Health Services*. HMSO, 1991. ISBN 0-11-886061-5.

141. *Transport: The Way Ahead* DOT, 1995.

142. *Transport: The Way Forward*. HMSO, 1996. ISBN 0-10-132342-5.

143. *The UK Environment*. HMSO, 1992. ISBN 0-11-752420-4.

144. *United Kingdom Environmental Health Action Plan: Public Consultation Draft*. DOE/DH, 1995.

145. *Urban Waste Water Treatment (England and Wales) Regulations 1994*. SI No 2841.

146. *Waste Management Licencing Regulations, 1994*. SI No. 1056.

147. *Water: Nature's Precious Resource: An Environmentally Sustainable Water Resources Development Strategy for England and Wales*. NRA, 1994.

148. *Welsh Health: Annual Report of the Chief Medical Officer 1994*. WO, 1995. ISBN 0-75-041527-4.

149. *Welsh House Condition Survey*. WO, 1994. ISBN 0-75-041037-X.

150. *A Working Countryside for Wales*. Cm 3180. HMSO 1996. ISBN 0-10-131802-2.

151. *Working Together for Better Health*. DH, 1993.

152. *The Workplace (Health, Safety and Welfare) Regulations 1992*, SI No. 3004.

EC Directives

153. *Animal waste (90/667/EEC)*.

154. *Evaluation and control of the risks of existing substances. (93/793/EEC)*.

155. *Freedom of access to information on the environment. (90/313/EEC)*.

156. *Hazardous Waste (91/689/EEC)*.

157. *Hygiene of foodstuffs (93/43/EEC)*.

158. *Informing the general public about health protection measures in the event of a radiological emergency (89/618/Euratom)*.

159. *Large Combustion Plant Directive (88/609/EEC)*.

160. *Legal provisions applicable to various substances in List 1 of annex to 76/464. (86/280/EEC)*

161. *Limit values and quality objectives for cadmium discharges (83/513/EEC)*.

162. *Limit values and quality objectives for certain List I substances (90/415/EEC)*.

163. *Limit values and quality objectives for discharges of hexachlorocyclohexane (in particular lindane) (84/491/EEC).*

164. *Limit values and quality objectives for hexachlorobenzene (HCB), hexachlorabutadiene (HCBD), chloroform, isodrin, endrin, dieldrin and aldrin discharges (88/347/EEC).*

165. *Limit values and quality objectives for mercury discharges by the chlor.-alkali electrolysis industry (82/176/EEC).*

166. *Limit values and quality objectives for mercury discharges by sectors other than the chlor-alkali electrolysis industry (84/156/EEC).*

167. *Major accident hazards of certain industrial activities. (Seveso Directive) (82/501/EEC).*

168. *Packaging and packaging waste. (94/62/EEC).*

169. *Pollution caused by certain dangerous substances discharged into the aquatic environment of the Community (76/464/EEC).*

170. *Proposal for a Council Directive concerning the quality of water intended for human consumption. (COM(94) 612 final). OJ No C 131, 30.5.95, pp.5.*

171. *Protection of fresh, coastal and marine waters from nitrate pollution [Nitrates Directive] (91/676/EEC).*

172. *Quality of bathing water (76/160/EEC).*

173. *Quality of fresh waters for fish life (Freshwater Fish Directive) (78/659/EEC).*

174. *Quality of shellfish waters (Shellfish Waters Directive) (79/923/EEC).*

175. *Quality of water intended for human consumption (The Drinking Water Directive) (80/778/EEC).*

176. *Standardising and rationalising reports on the implementation of certain Directives relating to the environment (91/692/EEC).*

177. *Urban waste water treatment (91/271/EEC).*

Annex 3 Health for All Targets

Target 18: Policy on environment and health

By the year 2000, all Member States should have developed, and be implementing, policies on the environment and health that ensure ecologically sustainable development, effective prevention and control of environmental health risks and equitable access to healthy environments.

Target 19: Environmental health management

By the year 2000, there should be effective management systems and resources in all Member States for putting policies on environment and health into place.

Target 20: Water quality

By the year 2000, all people should have access to adequate supplies of safe drinking water and the pollution of groundwater sources, rivers, lakes and seas should no longer pose a threat to health.

Target 21: Air quality

By the year 2000, air quality in all countries should be improved to a point at which recognised air pollutants do not pose a threat to public health.

Target 22: Food quality and safety

By the year 2000, public health risks due to microorganisms or their toxins, to chemicals and to radioactivity in food should have been significantly reduced in all Member States.

Target 23: Waste management and soil pollution

By the year 2000, public health risks caused by solid and hazardous waste and soil pollution should be effectively controlled in all Member States.

Target 24: Human ecology and settlements

By the year 2000, cities, towns and rural communities throughout the Region should offer physical and social environments supportive to the health of their inhabitants.

Target 25: Health of people at work

By the year 2000, the health of workers in all Member States should be improved by making work environments more healthy, reducing work related disease and injury, and promoting the wellbeing of people at work.

Target 11: Accidents

By the year 2000, injury, disability and death arising from accidents should be reduced by at least 25%.

Annex 4 The UK Process

1. This annex describes the process of Ministerial, administrative and public consultation by which this plan has been put together. It is provided at the request of WHO/EURO to assist other countries with less experience of developing such plans.

Before public consultation

2. The DH is the normal lead Department for dealings with WHO. In exercising this function, DH consults the other UK Health Departments. However, the measures to be taken in developing, and later implementing, the UK NEHAP fall principally on DoE and the other UK Environment Departments. Accordingly, the then Secretary of State for Health wrote in January 1995 to the Secretary of State for the Environment proposing that the latter's Department take the lead in developing the UK NEHAP: he agreed.

3. As a separate issue, the Secretary of State for the Environment wrote to the Secretary of State for Health, with copies to other Ministers whose Departments would contribute to the development of the UK NEHAP, proposing that the UK accede to WHO/EURO's request that the UK accept the role of a pilot country. Among the principal points made were:

- being a pilot country would require the UK to develop its plan faster than would otherwise have been the case;

- the role would not impose additional burdens except to the extent of cooperating with other countries involved in the pilot process. The additional burden would fall on the DoE as the Department developing the plan; and

- as the host country to the 1999 Third European Conference on Environment and Health, it was incumbent on the UK to try to ensure a successful conference.

The proposal was agreed without dissent.

4. Once Ministers had agreed, a letter was sent from a senior official in DoE to colleagues in other Government Departments, including NIO, SO and WO because of their responsibilities for health and the environment in their areas, and within DoE, seeking contributions to the draft UK NEHAP, having first set out the background and explained what was required. Administrative arrangements were made for an existing interdepartmental group of senior officials, the Inter-Departmental Group on Public Health,

chaired by the CMO, to maintain oversight of progress.

5. A draft for public consultation was agreed first between officials of DoE and contributors, generally in bilateral discussions with contributors, but including others if appropriate. The consultation process included the territorial departments to take account of their responsibilities for environment and health. Finally the document was cleared with Ministers by the Secretary of State for the Environment writing to colleagues seeking their agreement to publish the draft for public consultation.

Launch arrangements and public consultation

6. The public consultation draft of the plan was issued on 2 August 1995. The Secretary of State for the Environment and the Secretary of State for Health joined in a foreword to the document and their two Departments issued separate news releases quoting their individual comments in announcing the publication. The news releases were supported by notes for editors briefly explaining the document and saying where free copies could be obtained.

7. Departments were assisted in the distribution of the public consultation draft by the Chartered Institute of Environmental Health which distributed copies to all local authority Chief Environmental Health Officers. Copies were also sent to leading environmental and health institutions and organisations and to anybody requesting a copy. A covering note to all recipients advised that responses would be made available for public inspection unless the respondent requested that the response be treated in confidence. In all, over 2000 copies were distributed.

8. The public consultation period closed on 27 October 1995. In all, 246 responses were received: only two asked not to be made available for public inspection.

Analysis of responses

9. The public consultation draft was meant to draw a response in what was essentially a new area (albeit that its component parts were not new). The process was therefore more open-ended than has been the case where an integrated policy was already well established.

10. The principal criticisms made by respondents to the consultation are set out below with a brief commentary. Both the criticisms and the commentaries have influenced the final version of the plan.

(1) *The plan contained no new policy initiatives: it was no more than a collation of existing policies.*

Environmental health is cross-sectoral: policies affecting it are developed by relevant Departments in accordance with many criteria, of which environmental health is only one, although the action plan will increase the weighting attached to environmental health.

(2) *The plan did not contain many targets, dates and costs for actions.*

The Public Expenditure Survey system constrains firm financial commitments to one year, although indicative figures may be given for the longer term. Moreover, a commitment to continue existing levels of expenditure is a positive feature (all expenditure being tested against a 'do nothing' alternative). Many targets that already existed were buried in the descriptive text and have been drawn out more clearly, and where targets were lacking they have been developed as far as possible. The BATNEEC system is automatically progressive and, in many cases, obviates the need for specific targets in a national plan.

(2) *The plan was not holistic: it did not set priorities or describe a means of doing so.*

Holistic environmental health is best implemented through local promotion within a national framework. Nevertheless, the revised plan has attempted to draw the components more together. But priorities are difficult to set, given that the UK has no gross problems. In the present state of knowledge, the benefits to health from further improvements to the environment are not reducible to a cost-health equation, although research to clarify the issues are part of the plan. Public consultation enables Ministers to take into account what the public perceives as priorities.

(4) *The plan did not address the fundamental issues of equity or sustainable development, or such wider questions as an integrated transport policy.*

An environmental health plan is not the place to tackle such fundamental issues which should be addressed on their own merits, but the plan does fully reflect established policy on them. As an example, the wider debate on transport policy has already been brought into the public domain[139, 140] and the plan takes account of the debate.

(5) *The plan did not show how it would be extended to local environmental health action.*

This criticism is misconceived because local authorities have autonomy in their role of responding to local environmental health conditions in accordance with their responsibilities and local wishes. A proper cause for criticism would have been a plan which purported to dictate to local authorities.

11. Despite the criticisms, the public consultation draft of the plan was welcomed by many respondents as the first comprehensive statement of current and planned environmental health measures in the UK, and one which would provide the basis for policy development and further measures in future.

Revising the plan in the light of consultation

12. All responses to consultation were read and the sections of the plan to which they referred were noted. Each chapter was then edited in the light of these responses, and the need for textual amendments and additions was noted in the text to inform those contributors with relevant policy responsibilities. Major issues arising from the consultation were discussed directly with relevant officials, who consulted Ministers if new policy issues were involved.

13. The text of each chapter was also edited to improve clarity, relevance, accuracy and presentation. The presentation of the actions within the plan was also improved. Particular attention was paid to making sure that variations in environmental health policies and systems in Northern Ireland, Scotland and Wales were explained in more detail in the revised plan. After editing, each chapter was circulated to relevant contributing officials for them to deal with any questions raised. Where appropriate, contributors were also given copies or extracts of relevant consultation responses. This process needed more than one iteration.

14. A chapter on noise pollution, which was not included in the EHAPE, was added at the suggestion of many respondents to consultation. The objective for this chapter was formulated from current Government policy in this area.

15. Once all chapters were complete the plan was re-circulated in near final form to senior officials and contributors for comment and amendment.

Outstanding issues were resolved bilaterally with relevant officials in other Government Departments.

Clearance of the plan with Ministers

16. When the text had been developed to the near final stage described in para 15 above it was submitted for broad approval, together with proposals for publication and launch of the document, to the Secretary of State for the Environment, who wrote to Ministerial colleagues seeking their agreement to publication. Further minor changes were made as a result of comments on the near final document.

Publication and launch of the final document

17. Following receipt of Ministers' approval, the UK NEHAP was published as this White Paper. On the same day, the plan was launched by statements to Parliament and press briefing. Press notices about the plan were issued to the media.

Annex 5 Responsibility for Environmental Health

Central government

1. No single Government Department is responsible for the whole environmental health function. However, the principal areas of environmental health are generally grouped under the following headings:

(1) **Health**

(a) responsibility for public health;

(b) responsibility for the health effects of environmental issues covering the microbiological and toxicology of the environment;

(c) communicable disease surveillance and control;

(d) health promotion;

(e) microbiological and toxicological safety aspects of food, water and the environment;

(f) provision of primary, secondary and tertiary health care services, that is, the NHS and social services;

(g) planning for response by Government and the NHS to those aspects of major accidents which bear on health.

(2) **Environment**

(a) housing;

(b) waste management;

(c) environmental protection, including air and noise pollution;

(d) water;

(e) sewerage and sewage disposal;

(f) building regulations;

(g) occupational health and safety;

(h) effect of work activities on general public.

(3) **Transport**

(a) transport related pollution;

(b) traffic accidents.

(4) **Home Departments**

(a) byelaw approvals;

(b) licensing;

(c) administration of justice;

(d) fire; and

(e) emergency planning.

(5) **Agriculture, Fisheries and Food**

(a) food composition, standards and labelling;

(b) animal health and welfare;

(c) food science and technological research;

(d) control of products of animal origin;

(e) safety evaluation of pesticides and veterinary products;

(f) environmental protection for and from agriculture (with D0E);

(g) protection of the marine environment.

(6) **Trade and Industry**

(a) consumer protection.

2. The role of Government Departments takes several forms. This includes

– the formulation of policy;

– drafting and processing of legislation;

– provision of guidance on the legislation, and in some areas enforcement; and

– the administration of the legislative provisions, including the coordination and consultation with local government through the mechanisms of the Local Authority Associations and such affected interested parties as consumer associations, industry and the general public.

3. The Government has established several executive agencies which directly provide environment and health-related services at local level. These include:

– National Health Service Executive (in England);

– National Health Service in Scotland Management Executive;

Environment Agency;

– Scottish Environment Protection Agency;

– Health and Safety Executive;

– Countryside Commission.

4. For some matters the Government has established organisations for monitoring environmental health services at local level. The organisations include:

- Drinking Water Inspectorate;

- Medicines Control Agency;

- Social Services Inspectorate;

- Meat Hygiene Advisory Service;

- Scottish Centre for Infection and Environmental Health.

Local government services

5. Within the UK there are currently 472 democratically elected local government units. Within these units the ultimate authority for policy and decision rests with the elected Council of each unit. The units in **England** are London Boroughs, Metropolitan Districts, and in the shire areas County, District and unitary Councils. Within **Northern Ireland** there are 26 unitary District Councils. Within **Scotland** there are 32 unitary District and Island Councils. Within **Wales** there are 22 unitary District Councils. The unitary councils in England, Scotland and Wales were established on 1 April 1996 and followed reviews of the appropriate local government structure in those countries. There remain a handful of structural changes still to be implemented in England over the next few years. Within England and Wales, gross expenditure on local government environmental health services was £508 million in 1993-94 (source: Environmental Health Statistics 1993-94, Chartered Institute of Public Finance and Accountancy (CIPFA), 1995).

6. In general the environmental health service is located at local authority (community) level. There is a general recognition in the UK that there are strong advantages in the core environmental health service operating at the community level where it is in close contact with the population it serves and the environmental problems which it faces. The environmental health service covers the following broad areas:

- local policy formulation;

- surveillance;

- provision of information/ publicity;

- investigation services;

- health education;

- enforcement.

7. Within this overall framework (except in Northern Ireland) services are provided in the following areas:

- waste management/recycling of waste materials;

- food safety;

- housing;

- epidemiological surveillance and evaluation;

- air quality management;

- occupational health and safety;

- water resources management;

- noise control;

- protection of the recreational environment;

- radiation health;

- port health controls at air and seaports;

- educational activities;

- promotional enforcement of environmental health quality standards;

- studies into the effect of environmental hazards;

- environmental impact assessment;

- planning;

- refuse collection;

- social services;

- petroleum sales licencing;

- pest control; and

- pollution control.

8. The UK has officers with specialised training in environmental health who are recognised as constituting a specific professional group called Environmental Health Officers. The EHO is not only qualified at graduate level but must also have completed a period of compulsory practical training in the environmental health profession. EHOs are required to maintain their level of professional competency.

9. EHOs are mainly employed by the local authority at District Council level, although an increasing number of EHOs are employed by central government departments and industry. As professionally trained officers, EHOs are concerned with administration, inspection, education and regulation in respect of environmental health. They act as a public arbiter of environmental health standards, maintaining close contact with the community. They develop professional standards and apply them in

environmental health. A vital function is to maintain effective liaison with other professional officers who have a contribution to make in the promotion of environmental health in its widest sense.

10. An EHO within the public service should have the following basic functions:

(a) improving human health and protecting it from environmental hazards;

(b) maintaining public health, including the control of communicable diseases, food poisoning and infestation;

(c) enforcing environmental legislation;

(d) developing liaison between the inhabitants and the Local Authority, and between the local and higher levels of administration;

(e) acting independently to provide advice on environmental matters;

(f) initiating and implementing health education programmes to promote an understanding of environmental principles.

11. The other professionals with whom liaison is appropriate include physicians, microbiologists, public analysts, civil building and sanitary engineers, veterinarians, health and safety enforcement professionals, consumer protection officers, water engineers, scientists and staff of the pollution inspectorates.

12. A total of some 15,600 staff are employed in local authority environmental health services in England and Wales. As an example, in 1993-94 this figure included about:

5,200   Environmental Health Officers;
2,100   Specialist Technical Assistants;
1,500   Technical Assistants; and
600   Scientific Officers.

Other staff were employed as Dog Wardens, Pest Control Operatives, students, manual workers and in administration (source: Environmental Health Statistics 1993-94, CIPFA, March 1995).

13. The combination of centrally derived legislation, with locally accountable, professionally qualified service providers to take both a proactive and reactive approach to existing problems and developing problems, provide the framework for promoting:

• provision of easy access to an assured supply of safe water for every home;

• control of microbiological and chemical contamination of food and water supplies;

• regular collection and safe disposal of waste;

• control of air pollution hot spots;

• prevention of accidents at work, on the road and in the home;

• land use planning and control, as a means of preventing exposure of communities to pollutants in air, soil and water; and

• development of plans for prevention of and response to natural disasters and major industrial and nuclear accidents.

14. In recognising and encouraging the role of local government in providing environmental health services that are flexibly adapted to the needs of local populations, and to establish appropriate inter-sectoral infrastructures and adequate financial provision at those levels, the UK government has published *The Health of the Nation for Environmental Health*[66], which relates to England alone.

Annex 6 Housing Fitness Standard and Housing Condition

1. The **housing fitness standard** provides a statutorily enforceable set of minimum health and safety requirements deemed necessary for a dwelling to be fit for human habitation. These provide that a dwelling house should:

- be free from serious disrepair;

- be structurally stable;

- be free from dampness prejudicial to the health of the occupants;

- have adequate provision for heating, lighting and ventilation;

- have an adequate supply of wholesome water and an effective system for the draining of foul waste and surface water;

- have a suitably located WC, bath or shower and wash-hand basin; and

- satisfactory facilities for the preparation and cooking of food.

In Scotland, the broadly similar position is the Tolerable Standard, which sets out the minimum requirements a dwelling must have to be classified as suitable for habitation.

2. A quinquennial survey of housing – the *English House Condition Survey*[39] – is undertaken and the findings published. The next survey will start in 1996. The survey provides the major source of information to assist Government in the development and monitoring of policies directed towards the repair and improvement of the housing stock. The first Scottish House Condition survey was undertaken in 1991 and the results published by Scottish Homes in 1993[117]. A second survey is planned for 1996.

3. Means tested house renovation grants help those most in need in private sector housing with essential repairs and improvements. In Scotland, the current grant system is different: a general reform is proposed but there is no indication yet of the legislative timetable.

Annex 7 The Pilot Country Project and the NEHAPS Task Force

Establishing the Pilot Project

1. In view of the importance attached by the participants in the Helsinki Conference to the development of NEHAPs, WHO/EURO decided to set up a programme to help member countries develop their NEHAPs. The programme has four priority action areas:

(i)   NEHAP pilot project;

(ii) international actions on common and transfrontier issues in support of NEHAPs;

(iii) projects in support of countries in transition; and

(iv) development of environmental health action plans at the local level.

The four areas complement and support one another but the pilot project is seen as the main international action that will assist countries in developing their NEHAPs. It will generate the knowledge and practical experience which many countries feel they lack and which is important in developing their action plans. It should also help maintain the impetus which the Helsinki Conference gave to environmental health and help ensure that there is real progress to report at the Third European Conference on Environment and Health planned for 1999 in London.

2. Six countries were invited by WHO/EURO to act as pilot countries. They were chosen to give a representative spread in terms of geography and economic circumstances. The UK was among those invited ; the other countries were Bulgaria, Hungary, Italy, Latvia and Uzbekistan. The governments of all the pilot countries agreed to make the necessary commitment of resources to complete their NEHAPs by mid-1996. The project itself is scheduled for completion by the end of 1997.

3. A steering committee for the project was set up consisting of representatives of the pilot countries. At the first meeting of the steering committee (Budapest, January 1995), the pilot countries agreed to share experience, "to learn by doing" and not to wait until the end of the project before making their experience, in the form of guidance, available to all the countries in the European Region. They also agreed that their NEHAPs would follow the format set out in the EHAPE[42] as closely as possible so that they would

clearly be seen as a set of readily comparable examples which could act as models for non-pilot countries. At the request of WHO/EURO pilot countries agreed to include a description of their intra-governmental and administrative processes to assist countries less familiar with such processes.

4. Many of the countries of Central and Eastern Europe, and including three of the pilot countries (Bulgaria, Hungary and Latvia), are committed to preparing and implementing National Environmental Action Plans (NEAPs) as part of the agreement reached at the Environment for Europe Conferences held in Dobris Castle in 1991 and in Lucerne in 1993 under the auspices of the UNECE. An OECD/UNECE task force provides technical assistance to the countries concerned.

5. The Helsinki Conference agreed to establish the EEHC to act both as a focus for follow-up actions and as a coordinating mechanism for the activities of all the international agencies, including the funding agencies, with interests in environment and health in the European Region. The membership of the EEHC consists of representatives of eight countries, the Commission of the European Union, and all the relevant international agencies. Four of the countries (including the UK) were nominated by the WHO and four by the UNECE. The current chairman is Sir Kenneth Calman, the Chief Medical Officer in the DH.

6. At its first meeting in March 1995, the EEHC endorsed the WHO's strategy for following-up the agreements reached at the Helsinki conference and, in particular, the four priority action areas (see paragraph 1 above). To assist the EEHC in its work and to foster collaboration between the main partner organisations, including the financing institutions, the remit of the steering committee for the pilot project was extended and it was re-designated the NEHAP Task Force. The pilot project remains the principal interest of the Task Force but it assists the WHO in the other priority action areas and individual members of the committee, in particular the chairman, participate in activities in these areas. The chairman of the Task Force reports to the ECHE at each of its meetings progress on the pilot project and contributes to the report on the other elements of the NEHAPs programme.

7. The EEHC also recommended that there should be the closest possible collaboration between the NEAP and NEHAP task forces and between those responsible for the NEAPs and NEHAPS at the country level. Such collaboration was given further impetus by the Third Ministerial Conference on the Environment for Europe held in Sofia, Bulgaria in October 1995.

Experience of the NEHAP Pilot Project

8. The experience of the pilot countries indicates that there are five key elements in the development of a NEHAP:

    (i)   the Government's decision to develop the NEHAP;

    (ii) defining the basic strategy and preparing a work plan;

    (iii) the drafting process;

    (iv) public consultation/participation, involving all the relevant interests; and

    (v) developing and adopting the final version of the action plan.

These elements should not be seen as prescriptive but rather as a guide. Countries would still have to follow procedures which took account of the political, social, administrative and economic circumstances in their particular countries. The experience of the pilot countries in developing their NEHAPs (and NEAPs) is currently being distilled into a guidance document for other member countries. Further guidance on specific topics are planned (for example, on the integration of environmental health policies into national development strategies; and on environmental health financing).

9. The planning process in countries throughout the European Region is likely to have many points in common and the formats are likely to be similar since most will be based on the EHAPE[42]. However, the content of the NEHAP will vary depending on national circumstances and priorities and the selection of the countries to be pilot countries was made, in part, to ensure that a range of NEHAPs with different contents would be available as models for other countries.

10. As well as guidance documents and the NEHAPs of the six pilot countries, the pilot project includes holding consultation meetings where all the participating countries can share their experience and learn from the examples of the pilot countries. The first of these consultation meetings was held in Sofia in September 1995 and dealt primarily with the planning process. Further consultation meetings are planned to review progress in the development of NEHAPs throughout the European Region and to continue the sharing of experience.

International actions on common and transfrontier issues in support of NEHAPs

11. Many countries will have to address transfrontier issues in their NEHAPs and the same problems often occur in many different countries. For these reasons working together and sharing expertise can be beneficial. Facilitating such cooperation and capacity building are among the most valuable forms of assistance that an international organisation can provide for its members. Clearly this kind of mutual help is already an important aspect of the NEHAP pilot project but other supportive activities are also an important part of the overall programme.

12. Sub-Regional groups have come together, often at the initiative of one of the pilot countries, to discuss or collaborate on common and transfrontier issues. These are being supported by the WHO and are seen as a valuable way to encourage further, the development of NEHAPs and to provide information, advice and expertise in a cost-effective way.

13. Non-governmental organisations (NGOs) have an important part to play in developing and implementing NEHAPs. Thus NGOs can play a critical role in communicating with the public both in terms of representing the views of the public and in interpreting to the public the messages in the NEHAP. The economic sectors can assist in measures to implement NEHAPs through their investment strategies. However, some countries lack relevant experience and may need assistance from the WHO on how best to involve these sectors.

Projects in support of countries in transition

14. The countries concerned have limited national resources and limited ability to repay any external support received from international funding institutions. They face very difficult decisions therefore on how best to use the limited resources which are likely to be available to them for developing and implementing their NEHAPs. The WHO has explored with the World Bank how best to help countries in transition to define their environmental health priorities and investment strategies. Three major areas of cooperation have been

identified where the WHO and financial institutions such as the World Bank can assist and achieve maximum gain:

(i)   support in developing NEHAPs;

(ii) improving the environmental health institutional infrastructure; and

(iii) remedying priority environmental health problems.

The intention is that a programme of country projects should address these areas using bilateral and multilateral funds.